Published in cooperation with
The Institute for Psychohistory

Adolf Hitler:
A Family Perspective
by
Helm Stierlin

THE PSYCHOHISTORY PRESS
A Division of Atcom, Inc., Publishers

2315 Broadway • New York, New York 10024

4

Library of Congress Catalog Card Number: 76-23919

International Standard Book Number: 0-914434-02-0

To the Memory of my
Father and my Brother
Gerhard—two among the
millions who under
Hitler's reign found an
untimely death.

In every cry of every Man,
In every Infant's cry of fear,
In every voice, in every ban,
The mind-forg'd manacles I hear.
                    William Blake

CONTENTS

8

Helm Stierlin, M.D., Ph.D.

Helm Stierlin, M.D., Ph.D., is presently Chief of the Abteilung für Psychoanalytische Grundlagenforschung und Familientherapie, Universität Heidelberg, Germany. Before returning to his native Germany in 1974, he worked at various psychiatric hospitals in the U.S., at the National Institute of Mental Health in Bethesda, Md.—serving for some time as Acting Chief of its Adult Psychiatry Branch—and held academic positions at the John Hopkins University and the University of Maryland in Baltimore. Also, he served at the Faculties of the Washington Psychoanalytic Institute and Washington School of Psychiatry. His numerous publications in psychoanalysis, psychiatry and family theory include "Conflict and Reconciliation" (Doubleday, 1968) and "Separating Parents and Adolescents" (Quadrangle, 1974).

Foreword

It has been the fate of the present older generation to live through decades of mass murder and rampant sadism unparalleled in history. Just as science freed man from the hazards of many diseases and enabled him to bend nature to serve his ends, human nature became humankind's greatest enemy. Hitler and Stalin were the dual apotheoses of evil beyond comprehension. Helm Stierlin, among the most astute and creative of contemporary psychiatrists, has applied his clinical acumen and new conceptual tools to help unravel one of the period's—indeed of history's—most puzzling mysteries, a mystery beyond solution but which it is imperative that we seek to understand as fully as possible—the origins of Hitler's distorted personality and magnetic hold over millions of followers. We are herein afforded new insights into how the forces that produced this malignancy of the European body and spirit developed over several generations, and how the transactions within his natal family help explain the destructive force that emanated from him to envelop almost all of the Germanic world. Dr. Stierlin's thesis not only fascinates but provokes, and in the process fosters our understanding of other embittered, paranoid, and dangerous individuals.

Hitler and his deeds will haunt mankind for millennia unless an atomic holocaust, an offshoot of the weapon invented to defeat him, snuffs out the human race and its memories. He was not only responsible—as few in history have been solely responsible—for the planned extermination of millions of Jews and Poles and for the deaths of tens of millions who died in the ensuing war, but also for bringing an abiding disillusionment in the humanity of the human species. When the country of Goethe, Schiller, Mann, Bach, Beethoven, and Kant could be swayed to approve if not participate in massive genocide and to close its eyes to the practice of mass sadism, it became apparent that civilized behavior is but a thin veneer for a significant proportion of people. Christianity, the primary ethical force in the western world, suffered a devastating blow when it became apparent that its beliefs, teachings, and dictates as well as many of its vicars failed in the very heartland of Christian piety. For many, disbelief in the existence of God became preferable to belief that their God could permit such cruelty and suffering. Of course, there were those who stood their ground to defy Evil, and to die rather than countenance it, and there were millions willing to defend their countries against the spread of defilement of humankind. Yet the infection of the human spirit spread rapidly and widely. It has been difficult for most of us even to remember the origins and nature of the social plague that beset western civilization. We do not want to recall the horror or even its extent. We may hate the perpetrators, but as part of the human race we are also deeply ashamed—and afraid.

Pained, ashamed, afraid—we have difficulty focusing upon what Hitler and Hitlerism have meant to our ideas of mankind, humanity, religion, and personality development. It is less painful to plumb the economic, political, and social forces involved in the appearance and rise of Hitler. Studies of such forces are necessary and, as the Marshall Plan has shown, of great value in helping counter the rise of political movements of desperation. Still, even though we will never fully comprehend how Hitler came to be, it is also essential that we seek to understand the psychological issues involved—his childhood development, the influence of his family environment, the adolescent years of identity diffusion, the transformation that occurred at the end of the First World War. Our vulnerability is proportionate to our ignorance. It is important that, guided by studies such as Stierlin's, we seek to re-create from what is known about Hitler's childhood and youth and from what we have learned from the study of others with similar paranoid and sadistic tendencies what gave rise to this fanatic who was able to promote a devotion in others even though it led away from their religious and cultural ideals to embrace behavior totally antonymous to them.

We know and will know little about Hitler for several reasons. In part, because he emerged from the anonymity of a lower-middle class family—an unremarkable child of an unremarkable family, very much in contrast to Churchill, Roosevelt, and DeGaulle. In part, because his actual life has not only been obscured by a carefully constructed mythology, but also because he and his henchmen went to great pains to eradicate portions of his past. I do not know how much of Hitler's past was obliterated, or like his dark hair that became blond, altered; but I know that efforts were made, and that even Dr. Stierlin's carefully researched book shows that the efforts were successful as far as Hitler's record as a soldier is concerned. I shall tell how I know, and how the Nazi efforts to change the record had a profound influence on my life.

My father-in-law, Professor Karl Wilmanns, was Chairman of the Department of Psychiatry in Heidelberg when the Nazis took over the government. As an ardent anti-Nazi, he had disclosed something about Hitler he had learned as the chief military psychiatrist for Baden during World War I. He knew from records he had seen that the Nazi statement that Hitler had been blinded by poison gas was a fabrication. According to the hospital record, Hitler, after having been buried by a shell blast, suffered from hysterical blindness during which he had a vision of the Virgin. Because of the fear that Professor Wilmanns might have documents about Hitler's blindness in his possession, as well as because of his outspoken stand against National Socialism, he was immediately placed in "protective custody" and his home was searched repeatedly. As soon as her father was released from prison, my wife left Germany and eventually reached Baltimore where we met.

To the important task of penetrating the origins of Hitler's personality and his unusual capacities to pervert the ethics of millions, Dr. Stierlin has brought new approaches based not only upon recent developments in dynamic psychiatry but also upon his own contributions derived from studies of disturbed adolescents and their families. He focuses attention on the critical importance of the transactions in a person's natal family in shaping his personality and future life, indeed, upon the influence of family transactions across the generations upon the emergent child. Here, for example, he emphasizes the importance of Klara Hitler's (Adolf's mother) deprived childhood, and her early extrusion from her family to become the housekeeper-mistress of her future harsh and neglectful husband, and how these circumstances led Klara first to cater to her son and bind him to her, and later to delegate him to provide some meaning to her life (and, perhaps, to live out her repressed rage and avenge her). Alois Hitler, Adolf's father, an illegitimate son of a servant girl, furnished a pattern of self-betterment, having become a minor official and one of the petit bourgeoisie, but he was distant to his young third wife and brutal to Adolf whom he beat daily and sometimes mercilessly. He instilled bitterness, hatred, and a need for vengeance in Adolf Hitler, as well as the fate of being his mother's delegate that Dr. Stierlin has emphasized—and, perhaps the delegation of being her avenger. As Alois Hitler's mother had been a maid in a Jewish household and received a stipend from the family after Alois was born, it seems credible. that Alois was thought to be half Jewish, whether he was or not. It is conceivable that in defending his motherland from the Jews, Hitler was displacing his fantasies of defending his mother from the father he hated, but against whom he felt powerless. His last testament bears witness to his paranoid aggrandizement of the Jews, who, he believed, had managed to destroy him in the end despite his slaughter of six million of them. Thus, we may wonder, in contrast to Dr. Stierlin, if Hitler's father rather than his mother's Jewish physician may not have been the prime source of his implacable antisemitism.

Although the study focuses on Hitler, Dr. Stierlin has in the process furnished an excellent example of the application of his studies of the importance of the manner in which adolescents separate from their parents. Psychoanalytic psychology under the influence of Spitz, Mahler, and others has come to recognize that the young child's separation and individuation from the mother form a major developmental task, and that the vicissitudes of the process are a major factor in shaping the child's personality. Dr. Stierlin, along with others interested in family therapy, has a more transactional orientation than most psychoanalysts and considers the interaction of all family members on one another and thereby upon the nature of the separation-individuation process. Further, he recognizes that the process continues into or through adolescence, and has carefully studied and clarified the adverse effects of parents continuing to bind the adolescent to them in various ways, or to use the adolescent as their delegate, or to expel the adolescent from the family because of the needs of one or both parents or to maintain a family pseudoequilibrium.

Unfortunately, it is likely that many readers captivated by the study of Hitler's childhood and youth and by Dr. Stierlin's intriguing hypotheses may fail to appreciate the important contribution to personality development and to psychopathology

contained in this study of Hitler. Dynamic psychiatry has been
focusing increasingly on the importance of the family transactions
in shaping and misshaping the personalities of its offspring, and on
the transmission of familial influences extragenetically as well as
genetically. In this small volume Dr. Stierlin has again
demonstrated that he is one of the major contributors to the
emerging orientation, and one of the most stimulating thinkers in
contemporary psychiatry.

Theodore Lidz, M.D.
Professor of Psychiatry,
Yale University

INTRODUCTION

Why ever more volumes on Hitler when, as one expert estimates, more than 50,000 serious works, hundreds of them books, exist by now? The answer is simple: Hitler has become a nodal point for enduring questions about history, politics, ethics, and human psychology, questions with which we all grapple. The more we learn about Hitler, the more these questions stir us. Recently, my seven-year-old daughter sharpened them for me when she asked: Was Hitler the most evil man there ever was?

In trying to answer her, I began to recall how Hitler had entered my own life. That happened about forty years ago when I was roughly her age. I remember a rally of brownshirts in a park in Stettin, my home town (which was then capital of Pomerania and now belongs to Poland). Peter von Heydebreck, one of Hitler's SA chieftains, was visiting from Silesia and holding a review. One-armed and full of pride, he was sitting astride a horse which cantered in front of the assembled SA men and trampled the nearby rosebushes underfoot. Even now, no other image of omnipotence matches for me that of Peter von Heydebreck on horseback, casually trampling the roses. A short time later I heard of Heydebreck's death; Hitler, I learned, had had him shot as a traitor. For Heydebreck, along with several hundred others, was murdered on June 30, 1934, in the "Night of the Long Knives," during which Hitler eliminated many SA leaders and other—seeming or real—enemies of the Nazi movement. Heydebreck had lost his arm in the war, had led his own guerrillas against the Poles in 1919, and throughout had enjoyed Hitler's respect. As late as early June 1934, Hitler had ordered a village in Silesia named in his honor.

A year or two afterwards I almost saw Hitler. I was in a crowd that lined the tracks on which his train was expected. I still remember the soaring, ecstatic noise when the train finally passed by; but Hitler himself eluded me, since he was facing the crowds on the other side.

But of course I saw him countless times in newsreels and heard his voice over the radio—that voice which initially sounded so modest, so subdued, so pleading even, and which then became shrill and rasping with hate.

And Hitler was ever present after the war broke out in 1939. That war exposed me, then twelve years old, to endless appeals to be hard, to be self-sacrificing, to be proud, to be a true German, but, most important, to follow him, Hitler, blindly: *"Wer auf die Fahne des Führers geschwört, hat nichts mehr, was ihm selber gehört*" (He who swears by the Führer's flag forfeits all he owns).

As the war dragged on, it ceased to be mainly a matter of slogans, appeals, and victory news. American and British bombers attacked Stettin and, along with my classmates, I served in the city's air defense as an antiaircraft gunner. Classes in my high school, though, went on, now alternating with adolescent "war games" that somehow had become real. When one night large parts of Stettin were set afire, the excitement over playing soldier fused with a feeling of relief at the thought that a dreaded mathematics test, scheduled for the next morning, would be cancelled.

As my adolescence unfolded, the holocaust spread. When the war ended, I was near Pilsen in today's Czechoslovakia, a member of Hitler's beaten army. Fleeing the advancing allies, I reached Germany and stumbled into what only a day or two before had been the concentration camp of Buchenwald. I remember a talk with one former inmate who, emaciated and still in his prisoner's garb, shared with me the food he had received from liberating American troops while he hinted at what he had witnessed and endured. Not far away, townspeople and former SS-guards were digging graves for as yet unburied victims.

That was almost thirty years ago. But, clearly, it was all part of the experience that caused me to write this essay on Hitler.

Still, I would not have written it, had it not been for my experiences as psychoanalyst, family researcher, and family therapist. As such, I came to observe more and more families (in some cases including three generations)—broken families as well as overcohesive ones, families with neurotic, psychotic, psychosomatic, or delinquent members, as well as so-called "normal" families. Increasingly, I studied the deeper and mostly covert forces that shaped these families' lives, and gradually I developed a conceptual framework within which these forces could be understood.

Within the past few years, four foci of interpretation have emerged. While seemingly disparate, they are all derived from one basic, albeit emerging, family perspective. These are (1) the drama of separating parents and adolescents, (2) the artist's embroilment in liberative and self-destructive processes, (3) the dynamics of shame, guilt, and loyalty in family relations and, finally, (4) the power of group fantasies and family myths.

As I read more on Hitler, I realized that all these foci had their bearing on him as well as on my patients. As a result, the plan for this book germinated: Hitler could possibly serve as a test case for my family conceptions, i.e., could exemplify deeper, if extreme, aspects of human relations. At the same time, I felt, these conceptions could illuminate Hitler.

Two obstacles, though, both formidable, threatened my project. First, not being an historian, I had to rely on the works of other researchers. Yet, in mulling over their observations and conclusions, I often felt trapped in mazes of contradictory claims and inferences. Second, and related to the above, there was the fact that many important family data on Hitler have been lost, or exist only in questionable form. Here I think, above all, of data revealing a family's emotional climate, the members' shared fantasies, their often unstated expectations, needs, ambivalences, and loyalties—data that I hold to be central for any deeper understanding of families. Hitler's sparse references in *Mein Kampf* and elsewhere mislead us here as often as do the latter-day reminiscences of neighbors, of his boyhood friend Kubizek, of teachers, and others who knew—or pretended to know—him and his family. Yet, these data constitute, by and large, the evidence on which Hitler's biographers must draw. (So far, I have been unable to find even a single letter exchanged by Hitler's parents, which in turn might have allowed a glimpse into their marital relationship.)

There was no easy way around these obstacles. I had to work with the existent data, spotty and inconclusive as they often were. Luckily, I received the help of two historians—Professors Rudolph Binion of Brandeis University, and Eberhard Jäckel of Stuttgart—whose studies on Hitler are, in my opinion, outstanding. Both scholars read the manuscript of this book. Binion particularly, whose own research I found invaluable, alerted me to various inaccuracies, controversies, and open-ended questions, and even improved on my English. Professor Jäckel permitted me to use his as yet unpublished collection of Hitler documents containing all of Hitler's writings and recorded utterances up to the year 1924, and kindly allowed me to reproduce and analyze an as yet unpublished poem which Hitler wrote as an adolescent. But even though I benefited from these and other scholars' help, I often had only my intuition and psychological and psychoanalytical experience upon which to draw.

In the light of all the above, my objectives for this short book are limited. I take up only those features in Hitler's life and impact which are highlighted by my own interests and conceptions, and thus omit much that is important. Specifically, I bypass many of those political and social events that need to be considered in a historical context. Nonetheless, I believe my essay illuminates what so far has remained most obscure and controversial about Hitler—his motivational dynamics or, if you wish, his human dimension, and how this resonated with the condition and the needs of the German people.

The four main foci mentioned earlier determined the book's organization. The first chapter outlines the main known facts on Hitler's development and family, and then proceeds to summarize the existing psychoanalytic interpretations. The second chapter introduces us to Hitler's adolescent separation drama. Here I depict Hitler as the bound delegate of his mother, applying a viewpoint I have expanded elsewhere (1974c). In the third chapter I show how Hitler, as an artist of sorts, grappled with conflicts his family bequeathed him. As an artist, he turned Germany and the Western world into a gigantic participatory theater, destroying, in the process, himself and much of the theater too. In the next chapter I trace the dynamics of guilt, shame, and loyalty in Hitler's psychological make-up and human relations, dynamics that also spring from formative family experiences. In the final chapter I take up some of the group processes that Hitler enacted with his followers. Here, too, a family viewpoint is central.

Helm Stierlin, M.D., Ph.D.

ACKNOWLEDGMENTS

In addition to Rudolph Binion and Eberhard Jäckel, already mentioned in the Introduction, I owe special thanks to Lloyd deMause and John Toland for letting me use their unpublished sources or formulations. My wife Satu Stierlin, Margaret Singer, Kay Scheuer, Alexander Mitscherlich, Lyman Wynne, and Ivan Boszormenyi-Nagy were foremost among those who inspired or helped me—as friends, critics, or editors—in writing this book. And once again I acknowledge Audrey Jorday's invaluable and generous secretarial and research assistance, given under trying circumstances.

Helm Stierlin

CHAPTER I

HITLER REVEALED AND CONCEALED

Today, thirty-one years after his death, we see Adolf Hitler in widening perspectives. But these perspectives pose new challenges and problems. As scholars have unearthed new data, his personality has grown more complex. Initially, biographers and historians saw him as just a monster, madman, or opportunist. Such views were soon found simplistic, and in one of the latest and most thoroughly researched biographies—by J. C. Fest (1973/1974)—Hitler emerges as an extraordinarily complex, albeit evil, genius who mustered many talents and skills.

But while biographers have elaborated his intricate character and life course, they have also found him the mirror and catalyst for the longings, conflicts, and anxieties of his age: a "vessel" for supraindividual forces that could have converged on someone else. We thus confront two seemingly opposed perspectives on Hitler, one emphasizing the man's uniqueness, the other his ordinariness. Which perspective prevails depends, essentially, on how we focus our searching telescope. When we focus on Hitler's uniqueness, his role as mere vessel blurs; when we emphasize his "vessel" role, we risk missing his specific, and perhaps decisive, contributions. Yet, depending on the focus we choose, we do learn to see different facets of the lesson that his history offers, and to account differently for the crimes that resulted.

In the following, I shall try to reconcile the above two perspectives—to consider Hitler's uniqueness, but also to view him as a link in a wider chain; to see him as mover and moved, as victimizer and victim.

As a start, let me list some of those features of Hitler that most tax our understanding. Among these I count his high energy level, his passion for power, his force of will, his sense of certainty, his belief that he was chosen by destiny, his radicalism, his hatred of Jews, his craving for ever more *Lebensraum*,[1] his—seeming or real—quest for self-destruction, and his ability to recruit followers. What, we ask, are the deeper determinants of these traits and motives? To find an initial answer and to lay a base for what follows, we turn, in accord with our chosen vantage point, to his family and formative years.

HITLER'S FAMILY AND FORMATIVE YEARS IN OVERVIEW

In the last few decades, historical researchers have left hardly a stone unturned in the effort to discover new evidence on Hitler's family and childhood. Still, there remain many gaps and controversies, and these bear on what I shall report. What follows owes much to the observations or conclusions of, among others, R. Binion (1973), B. F. Smith (1967, 1973), W. Maser (1971/1973), F. Jetzinger (1956), J. C. Fest (1973/1974), E. Jäckel (1969/1972), and A. Kubizek (1953). The first four—two Americans, one German, and one Austrian—researched, weighed, and consolidated the original sources on Hitler's family and youth. Fest, a German journalist, although not engaged in primary research, has authored one of the most recent and exhaustive Hitler biographies. Jäckel, a German historian, has shared with me many of his as yet unpublished data. Kubizek, Hitler's boyhood friend, published his reminiscences on Adolf after the end of World War II. The latter, though they reveal their author as a naive admirer, unreliable witness, and unrepentant, if passive, Nazi, are valuable as an intimate portrait of Hitler as adolescent. Of the above authors, I consider Smith, Binion, and Jäckel the most trustworthy. Inevitably, my account, like any other, selectively emphasizes the features in their work that I consider important.

Hitler's ancestors lived in the Waldviertel, an Austrian border area inhabited mostly by impoverished peasants. Here Hitler's father, Alois Schicklgruber, was born as the illegitimate son of a 42-year-old peasant woman, Maria Anna Schicklgruber. To this day it is uncertain who Alois' father was. It is possible—but unlikely—that he was Jewish, as Maria Anna is said to have worked, at one time, in a Jewish household, and to have received maintenance payments for the child, afterward, from her employer. When Alois was five years old, his mother married a certain Johann Georg Hiedler, the brother of Johann Nepomuk Hüttler (the spelling of Hiedler, Hüttler, and Hitler were used almost interchangeably). Several decades later—long after the death of Maria Anna Hiedler and Johann Georg Hiedler—Alois Schicklgruber legitimized himself in a local church register with the help of three illiterate witnesses and, as a result, adopted the name of Alois Hitler. He married three times and also had affairs with other women. He married his first wife, who was 14 years older than himself, when he was 36; his last, Klara Pölzl, married him when he was 47, and was 23 years his junior. Alois apparently took Klara into his household when she was 15. Before she—according to as yet undocumented evidence—became his common-law wife on August 10, 1884, she had served as his mistress, maid, and the nurse of his children. She was made pregnant by him about the time his second wife, Franziska Matzelberger, died. Klara became the mother of Adolf Hitler.

ALOIS HITLER

In his career, Alois achieved more than any other Hiedler or Hitler ever had. He worked hard and rose from the status of shoemaker to membership in the Austrian Frontier Guard, which served under the Austrian Ministry of Finance. After 1875, he worked as a "full inspector of customs." This insured him respectable status, a comfortable standard of living, and an ample retirement pension. The available photographs show a proud and imposing man.

Hitler's biographers note Alois' strict devotion to duty, and Smith, for one, reports his "genuine respect for other people's rights and real concern for their welfare."[2] He could be rough and heavy-handed but was by no means a fanatic and, on the whole, seemed tolerant. His interest in politics was strong; his political attitudes were anticlerical and liberal. Moments before he died of a heart attack while reading a newspaper, he is said to have lambasted "those blacks," as reactionary clericals were called. He liked to drink with his cronies in the village inn, but little bespeaks his having been an alcoholic. In his spare time, Alois loved to putter in his garden or farm, and he had a deep and abiding interest in bees and beekeeping.

KLARA HITLER

Klara was the seventh of eleven siblings, the daughter of poor peasant parents. After Alois had adopted the name of Hitler, she was in a legal sense his cousin. since she was Johann Nepomuk's granddaughter, and Alois was legally Johann Nepomuk's nephew. Whether she was also related by blood cannot be ascertained. A photo of her as a young wife shows a plain, apparently likeable country girl. Observers knew her as hard-working, quiet, unassuming, kind, and responsible. The historian, Smith, on whom I here rely most heavily, describes her as follows:

> Her life was centered on the task of maintaining her home and caring for her husband and the children of the family. She was a model housekeeper, who maintained a spotless home and performed her duties with precision. Nothing could distract her from her round of household toil, not even the prospect of a little gossip. Her home and the furthering of the family interests were all-important; by careful management she was able to increase the family possessions, much to her joy. Even more important to her than the house were the children. Everyone who knew her agreed that it was in her love and devotion for the children that Klara's life centered. The only serious charge ever raised against her is that because of this love and devotion she was over-indulgent and thus encouraged a sense of uniqueness in her son—a somewhat strange charge to be brought against a mother. The children did not share this view. Her stepchildren and her own offspring who survived infancy loved and respected their mother.[3]

KLARA'S AND ALOIS' MARITAL RELATIONSHIP

How did Hitler's parents perceive and affect each other? Here again, I rely strongly on Smith: "At home," he notes,

> He [Alois] was something more than a formidable character. He was master, and he impressed this fact upon every member of the household. He alone had the whole lot of them and he demanded the obedience and respect that he felt they owed him. Despite his monopoly of family power he was not a tyrant, nor did he poke and pry into every feature of family life. The household was there to serve

his needs while he provided the income for a better than average living and set the family tone. The bulk of his time was spent in long and irregularly timed tours of duty at the customs station; when he came home he wanted to eat and sleep without interference. When he wanted recreation he went to the tavern, but that was his own affair and did not concern the family. If, when he came home, things were out of line, his voice would generally set things right. If more was needed, then a box on an onstinate child's ear soon set matters straight. The judgment of a friend of later years who held that 'his bark was worse than his bite' was undoubtedly correct; his bluster was also bluff, but it succeeded completely.[4] the old man's dominance made him a permanent object of respect, if not of awe, to his wife and children. Even after his death his pipes still stood in a rack on the kitchen shelf, and when his widow wished to make a particularly important point she would gesture toward the pipes as if to invoke the authority of the master.[5]

Alois' dominance at home contrasts with Klara's submission. About her marital relations and status, Smith writes:

She seems to have lofty and hopeful dreams about her married life which were abandoned only slowly and painfully. The relationship in which Alois was both a status symbol and a husband left the girl in a confusing and helpless position. How much this ambivalence affected her outlook can be seen in the fact that she found it exceedingly difficult to accustom herself to playing the role of Alois' wife. Try as she might, the poor girl was unable to break herself of the habit of addressing Alois as 'uncle' until long after the marriage ceremony.[6,7]

ADOLF'S EARLY DEVELOPMENT AND FAMILY RELATIONS

Klara Hitler gave birth to three children in close succession. However, all died within a short time after the third birth, as is shown by the following chart:[8]

	Born	*Died*	*Age at time/death*
1. Gustav	5/17/1885	12/8/1887	2 yr. 7 mos.
(diphtheria)			
2. Ida	9/23/1886	1/2/1888	1 yr. 4 mos.
(diphtheria)			
3. Otto	1887	1887	approx. 3 days
(diphtheria)			
4. Adolf	4/20/1889		
5. Edmund	3/24/1894	2/2/1900	almost 6 yrs.
6. Paula	1/21/1896		

After the deaths of her first three children, Klara was once more relegated to what she had been before her marriage to Alois: a nurse to Franziska's children, a housekeeper, and cook. This changed only when she gave birth to another boy, Adolf Hitler.

When Adolf was born, the child was sickly, notes Smith, "and Klara lived in constant fear that he, too, would die in infancy. The baby never acquired a rugged constitution, but his mother's fears gradually abated . . . ."[9]

But while Klara's concern for Adolf's health and survival might have lessened, her investment in him remained strong. The available evidence indicates she stayed deeply devoted to him.

Very likely, Alois did not always take calmly Klara's devotion to her son. Although the evidence is spotty, we can assume that he resented Adolf as an intruder—as one who deprived him of Klara's attention and affection[10]—and that this was one of the reasons why he beat the boy, which he apparently did routinely and harshly.[10a] For example, William Patrick Hitler, the son of Adolf Hitler's half-brother, Alois, Jr.,

> . . . remembered his father telling him one time with considerable glee that when Adolf was about 11 years old he refused to put up with the maltreatment of his father any longer and resolved to run away from home with two other boys. The plan was to build a raft and float down the river. Preparations were already underway when the father got wind of it and went down to the river to find the boys engaged in their raft building. He was furious and beat Adolf so violently that when he returned home he was afraid that he had killed him, but Adolf survived.[10b]

And Adolf's sister Paula stated later (in an interview with John Toland):

It was especially my brother Adolf, who challenged my father to extreme harshness and who got his sound thrashings every day. He was a scrubby little rogue, and all attempts of his father to thrash him for his rudeness and to cause him to love the profession of an official in the state were in vain.[10c]

Given these conditions, it seems likely that Adolf feared and hated his father even though in *Mein Kampf* he professes his respect—though not love—for the latter. In the same work, he also hints at his early fear and hatred of Alois. For example, he elaborates on the miserable home life of lower-class families and, in so doing, seems to evoke memories from his own childhood.[11] We read:

In a basement apartment, consisting of two stuffy rooms, dwells a worker's family of seven. Among the five children there is a boy of, let us assume, three. . . . Quarreling and wrangling will very frequently arise. . . . But if this battle is carried on between the parents themselves . . . in forms which for vulgarity often leave nothing to be desired, then . . . the results of such visual instruction must ultimately become apparent in the children. The character they will inevitably assume if this mutual quarrel takes the form of brutal attacks of the father against the mother, of drunken beatings, is hard for anyone who does not know this milieu to imagine. At the age of six the pitiable little boy suspects the existence of things which can inspire even an adult with nothing but horror. . . . All the other things that the little fellow hears at home do not tend to increase his respect for his dear fellow men.[12]

It ends badly if the man goes his own way . . . and the woman, for the children's sake, opposes him. Then there is fighting and quarreling, and, as the man grows estranged from his wife, he becomes more intimate with alcohol. . . . When at length he comes home . . . drunk and brutal, but always parted from his last cent, such scenes often occur that God have mercy!

I have seen this in hundreds of instances. At first I was repelled or even outraged. . . .[13]

Even though it now seems unlikely that his father was alcoholic, Adolf's image of him as a brutalizing tyrant probably reflects authentic personal experience. Smith seems to confirm this when he writes "When he [father] arrived home in an irritable mood, the older children and his wife bore the brunt of his wrath. Klara was wise enough in the ways of her husband to move the infant out of harm's way whenever the danger flags were flying."[1][4]

ADOLF'S EARLY YEARS

When Adolf was born on April 20, 1889, the Hitler family had five members. Besides him, there were two half-siblings from the father's second marriage: Alois, Jr. and Angela. Edmund, Klara's fifth child, was born when Adolf was five years old, and Paula, her sixth and last, arrived two years later. Edmund died when he was not quite six years old, of measles, but Paula survived into adulthood and at later times served as Hitler's housekeeper. Of his siblings and half-siblings, Adolf seems to have been closest to Angela and Paula. When Angela later married, he loathed his brother-in-law, Leo Raubal. His half-brother, Alois, Jr., was a ne'er-do-well and remained—for his parents and Adolf—a source of embarrassment.[1][5]

As the father's place of work shifted repeatedly, the family changed residence several times until Alois retired in 1897 in Leonding, a small community just outside of Linz. While these moves might have unsettled the family members, no traumatic effect on Adolf is reported. Neither does the birth of his brother, Edmund, seem to have adversely affected the five-year-old Adolf.

Adolf did well in the two grade schools he attended. In one class picture, taken in 1899, he poses confidently in the middle of the upper row. But when he entered a *Realschule* (an Austrian version of the American high school) the following year, he failed. Twice he had to repeat a grade and another time he advanced only after a repeated examination. A change in schools in 1904—from the *Staatsrealschule* in Linz to the *Staatsoberrealschule* in Steyr near Linz—did not improve his academic performance. Almost all report cards called his diligence (*Fleiss*) uneven, and gave him failing grades in major subjects.

Hitler's failure at the *Realschule* has puzzled his biographers. An an explanation, they have pointed to a change in his peer relations. Whereas earlier he had been a leader, he was now an outsider; his fellow students kept their distance and Hitler found no friends among them. At the same time—to judge from what we read in *Mein Kampf*—his quarrels with his father intensified. Hitler attributed his school failure to his stubborn resistance to a father who tried to coerce him into the dull career of civil servant. But this explanation is unconvincing, as Adolf did no better in school after his father's death. Also, it is doubtful whether Alois ever took that much interest in his son's career, the more so as Adolf, by the time of his father's death, was not yet of an age to be under pressure to choose a career. Apart from the one thwarted attempt mentioned above, Adolf, in any case, never seems to have considered openly defying his father and leaving home—as his half-brother, Alois, Jr., did at the age of 14. It appears certain, however, that tensions between the father and Adolf mounted when Alois Hitler retired early at the age of 58. Gearing himself to a leisurely life of beekeeping and farming, he spent more time at home, yet also demanded more attention and obedience, and necessarily limited his son's freedom of movement. When his father died, Adolf, then 14, seemed not unduly grieved.[16] His lackluster performance at the *Realschule* continued for two-and-a-half years. Finally, "in disgust and self-indulgent lassitude," to use Fest's words,[17] he quit altogether.

Klara, we learn, worried about Adolf's school failure and tried to induce him to study and pursue a respectable career. But her actions seem to have contradicted what she said, for rather than confront him squarely she indulged him and supported his idle ways.

After Adolf had left the *Realschule*, the four remaining family members—Adolf, Klara, Paula, and Klara's sister, Johanna—shared quarters for more than two years in a flat on the Humboldtstrasse in Linz. This became Adolf's sanctuary, where he spent his hours "reading, drawing, and dreaming." His mother paid the bills and his sister Paula cleaned up after him. Hitler said later that at that period he lived as an eccentric (*Sonderling*). Apart from his mother and his boyhood friend and naive admirer, August Kubizek, his world was then nearly devoid of people. A seemingly ardent infatuation with a certain Stephanie was not even noticed by the girl. He behaved and dressed like a dandy ("complete with cane, top-hat, frock coat, and kid gloves"),[18] attended many theater and opera performances, and responded enthusiastically to Wagner's works. He appeared undisciplined, impetuous, unable to concentrate on any task, yet ready to blame others with righteous wrath for any frustration, always eagerly searching after new stimulations, and ever prone to retreat into fantasies—an emotionally and intellectually retarded adolescent, according to Binion. Yet later he told Kubizek that these were the happiest years of his life.

Finally, in 1908, Hitler moved to Vienna, where he stayed until

1913. He went there to study painting at the Academy of Fine Arts but, to his dismay, was twice rejected. (At the first examination—which required Hitler to visit Vienna in September 1907—only 28 of the original 113 candidates satisfied the examiners.)[19] He then succumbed to a shiftless life, made possible largely by money reaching him from his father's estate. After two-and-a-half years in Vienna, the would-be art student had become a homeless tramp with no worthwhile prospects, scurrying to get a bowl of hot soup, and making little if any effort to support himself.

In January 1907, when Adolf was nearly 18 years old and still living in Linz, his mother consulted a Jewish doctor named Eduard Bloch about a pain in her chest. The doctor diagnosed cancer and had one of her breasts removed. The cancer recurred, however, and Bloch—apparently with Adolf's agreement and probably with his encouragement—treated his mother with local applications of iodoform, i.e., frequently changed iodoform-drenched gauzes applied to the cancerous and putrefying wound. Such treatment, intended to be antiseptic, was then not uncommon, yet it was not only painful but—in the light of modern medical knowledge—ineffective and, if given in large and frequent doses, poisonous (due to the absorption of the chemical into the bloodstream). Klara died approximately seven weeks later. According to Bloch and other observers, Adolf was deeply grieved over her illness and death. Bloch declared in November 1938: " 'His attachment to his mother was deep and loving. He would watch her every movement so that he might anticipate her slightest need. His eyes, which usually gazed mournfully into the distance, would light up whenever she was relieved of her pain.' "[20] And Bloch recalls from the day of her burial on December 23, 1907: " 'In all my forty odd years of practice I had never seen a young man so broken by grief and bowed down by suffering as young Adolf Hitler was that day.' "[21]

After having attended her funeral and disposing of her estate, Hitler settled in Vienna. Several years later he moved into a so-called *Männerheim*—a home for single men (comparable to the YMCA)—in that city and subsisted mainly on the sale of his own hand-painted postcards. A fellow tramp by the name of Hanisch was his principal salesman until the two finally quarreled.

In 1913 Hitler moved to Munich, the capital of Bavaria. But there too he barely survived. He existed mainly by doing copywork for a commercial artist and sold his pictures in beer halls and from door to door. Then World War I broke out. Hitler, who had dodged the Austrian draft (and had thereby made himself subject to legal inquiries), now enthusiastically joined the ranks of the German army. During much of his career as a soldier he served as a dispatch runner, often exposing himself to danger. For his bravery he was decorated and respected by his superiors. As a soldier he was responsible, disciplined, and quite a different man from the painter of Viennese days. In the last months of the war he was blinded by poison gas. As he was regaining his sight at a military hospital in Pasewalk, the war ended with Germany's defeat. Hitler was then 30 years old.

THE PROSPECTS FOR PSYCHOLOGICAL ANALYSIS

The above overview summarizes the hard core of fact upon which Hitler's interpreters must necessarily depend. Yet to most of them, his early life appears in no way extraordinary. Smith speaks for many when he asserts that "In the deeds of the man as a youth there are few discernible traces indeed of evil genius."[22] And, unable to find even one report of a deliberately cruel act, he holds young Adolf to be "an essentially sympathetic figure."[23] "With a few exceptions, none conspicuous," he notes, "the young Adolf might have been born to any Austrian peasant family undergoing the transition to lower middle-class status as European social structures gradually adjusted to an industrial rather than an agrarian economy."[24] But Smith concedes that we must look to these beginnings "for the explanation [albeit partial] of how Hitler's weakness became strength and how romantic escapism was transformed into a quest for power and a demand for extreme solutions."[25]

I agree—and to seek an explanation, let us now turn to those authors who have tried to interpret Hitler within essentially psychoanalytic frameworks.

All of them, we notice at once, confront serious problems. For while they assume that early family relations stake out the narrow corridor in which a person's needs, motivations, and conflicts are decisively shaped, they also find that this corridor remains shrouded in darkness or ambiguity. For what frequently counts here are subjective experiences rather than objective facts and covert rather than overt features and processes. To do justice to these, we must often take a new look at available findings, including those that seem tangential or trivial. Yet in Hitler's case, this evidence is often circumstantial and remains open to doubt.

Furthermore, even as the research on Hitler yields such evidence, it raises new questions. For as an ever more complex

Hitler emerges, psychological theories have to catch up with his complexity and today, it appears, no one theory can encompass the whole man. Rather, each theory seems to cover only a segment of his personality or life. While many of these segments fit together, others do not. As this happens, we must reconsider our evidence and adopt different or wider perspectives.

With these considerations in mind, we turn to those perspectives which psychoanalytically-oriented researchers offer. Each derives from the hard core of findings that I have outlined and each selectively rearranges these findings, emphasizing some aspects and neglecting others. (Only one perspective introduces new data that call into question central assumptions about Hitler.) To the extent that these perspectives diverge, we are challenged to reconcile, modify, or discard them. Essentially, three major perspectives exist.

THE CLASSICAL OEDIPAL FORMULA

Insofar as each child, according to Freud, must pass the phallic phase, he must confront the oedipus complex. How he does so will shape his outlook on life and affect his growth, personal relations, and vulnerability to neuroses or psychoses. To be successful here, a boy must walk a narrow path. He needs a benevolent father with whom he can identify on a basis of admiration and trust. Yet he also needs a father whom he can perceive and (within limits) fight as rival. He needs a mother who cares for him intimately and protectively, and in the process stimulates—but does not overstimulate—his tender and erotic feelings, providing a valued image that may guide him to adult partners. But he also needs a mother who gradually detaches herself from him, and thus sets him free. Given this precarious balance of interpersonal forces, the oedipal passage may easily fail and subsequently cause arrest of growth and various forms of psychopathology. Thus, if the mother ties the boy to herself with excessive intensity, her later detachment from him will be experienced as a disabling and derailing withdrawal. But when the mother remains too distant, the child's base for a secure identity and for self-esteem may be weakened from the outset. When the father is not admired and loved, but overwhelmingly hated and feared, the boy lacks a model for trusting male identifications and the pull needed to detach him from his mother; yet, when the father remains passive and weak, he fails to provide an adequate rival for his son to fight. Elsewhere I have elaborated these varying oedipal constellations (1971).

When we turn to Hitler we find an oedipal pattern that fits this classical formula and that spells neurotic trouble—one whose main ingredients are an overgratifying mother and a brutalizing, "castrating" father. It constitutes the base on which psychoanalytic interpreters of Hitler tend to build their cases. Langer (1972), Bromberg (1971, 1974), and Waite (1965, 1971) are representative here. In accord with the above formula, they emphasize Hitler's sexual perversions (which even today are controversial and basically unsubstantiated: Hitler is said to have needed a woman to urinate or defecate on him in order to achieve full orgastic relief, and to have had voyeuristic inclinations), and his other difficulties with women (whom he had to keep at arm's length and in inferior positions), since these features seem to indicate an excessive castration anxiety, an early sexual overstimulation by (and fixation to) his mother, and a generally derailed male identity—features that would fit the above oedipal pattern.[26] Rightly or wrongly, Bromberg (1971), speculates that Hitler may have observed violent parental intercourse—presumably *a tergo*—and that his monorchism (only one testis in the scrotum)[27] underlay his deep sense of sexual inadequacy. In this way Bromberg illuminates such features as the adult Hitler's tense and rigid oratorical posture—in which his whole body came to resemble a phallus—and his aggressive, "castrating" stare, commented on by many observers including Speer (1971). All of these served, according to Bromberg, to counter the ever present castration threat; while J. Brosse (1972), along similar lines, explains Hitler's vegetarianism and distaste for smoking. (His father was an inveterate pipe smoker as well as meat eater, and Hitler, primarily because of the castration threat, had to guard against these symbolic vestiges of a masculinity that he craved, yet feared.)

Further, this perspective takes account of Hitler's guilt-ridden wish for, and struggle against, incest with his mother and her substitutes—as seemingly exemplified in the most passionate, and perhaps the only meaningful, relationship he ever had with a woman other than his mother: his quasi-incestuous affair with his half-niece "Geli" Raubal,[28] the daughter of his half-sister Angela.

But while it illuminates such traits as these, the above perspective tries, most of all, to account for Hitler's aggressive drive. This drive is viewed as the expression of a retaliatory fury that dates back to what transpired between Adolf and his castrating, brutalizing father, a fury displaced onto establishment figures and Jews; and it reflects a never-ending attempt to compensate for his inwardly felt weakness and sexual defectiveness: he had to be harder, crueler, more ruthless, and more iron-willed than anyone else. Further, this perspective accommodates, at least partly, Hitler's sadomasochism, as this appears tied to his (seeming or real) sexual immaturities and perversions. Blocked from normal sexual fulfillment, yet shamefully reeling under his deviant cravings, he had to resort here to vicarious experiences and compensatory ploys—e.g., feeding himself and his mass audiences with macabre images of slimy, perverted Jews raping blonde Aryan virgins.

But by itself the classical oedipal formula explains little, for it fails to account for the radicalism in Hitler's destructiveness, for his sense of uniqueness and mission, for his inflexible will, for his inordinate hatred of Jews, for his quest for *Lebensraum*, for his capacity to instill loyalty, and for other central features of his psyche. To account for at least some of these, psychoanalysts—particularly Waite (1965, 1971), Kurth (1950, 1947), and Brosse (1972)—focused on that aspect in his family relations that all researchers attest: his early closeness to, and indulgence by, his mother.

To an extent this closeness fits into an intensified oedipus complex, as it lays the basis for an incestuousness which could not but fuel his father's rivalry and increase his real or perceived threat as castrator. But this early closeness also implies more than the oedipal formula conveys. Several aspects, all bearing on the oedipal conflict, but also independently significant, stand out here.

There is, first, Klara's oral gratification of Adolf. As a baby Hitler was over-fed, as is evident from the only extant photograph of those years. Such early oral indulgence appears to be at the root of the enormous oral animus Hitler showed as an adult. Up to the time of his death in the *Reichskanzlei-Bunker*, he craved chocolate and cake and fought a constant battle against these because, as Führer, he could not afford a pot-belly. After major exertions or triumphs, too, he would gorge himself with sweets and then doze off blissfully like a happily satisfied baby. For example, within days of his triumphant defense at the trial following the *Putsch* of 1923 his weight rose to 170 pounds, and two months after his release he still "looked positively pudgy from the sweets that he ate in prison," according to the information which Binion summarizes.[29] Further, his conquest of land—*Lebensraum*—seemed fueled by oral greed. Once he had conquered territory he would never surrender it voluntarily; hence his stubborn, self-defeating refusal to yield militarily untenable positions. "*Wer hat, der hat*" (he who has, has), he is quoted as saying.

But such greed, it appears, was not the only effect of Hitler's early indulgence by and close relationship with Klara. His most basic defenses and conflicts seemed affected; not surprisingly, for such early closeness is known to interfere with many a child's age-appropriate psychophysiological differentiation and integration. Instead of experiencing conflicts he can manage, the child suffers an archaic, terrifying ambivalence. Caged into a closeness from which there is no escape, he loses all sense of autonomy. We have reason to believe that this triggers murderous wishes—i.e., wishes to bite, mutilate, and destroy the mother—wishes that may cause profound anxiety and guilt and then give rise to dissociation, splitting, or projection. The details of these need not concern us; M. Klein (1956, 1957) and her followers, among others, have adequately described them. Suffice it to say that such early vicissitudes may account for later ego defects, as well as inordinate aggression, projection, and self-destruction—traits that Hitler demonstrated. Brosse (1972) and Kurth (1947, 1950) especially, albeit in varying and sometimes ambiguous language, have postulated or implied such dynamics.

The early closeness also suggests a special type of symbiosis which some analysts believe accounts for Hitler's sense of uniqueness and strength. As long as he could maintain or recreate such symbiosis, he could exult in infantile omnipotence and invincibility; he could treat the world as his mother's extended womb. Kurth, especially, saw Hitler's success as an agitator to be a reenactment with mass audiences of the early symbiosis with his mother—e.g., of an increasingly orgastic mutual feeding process. While he "fed"—or, better, *force-fed*—these audiences with intoxicating slogans, he accepted from them a reciprocal "nourishment": the strength he needed to execute his mission.

ERICH FROMM'S PERSPECTIVE ON HITLER:
A CASE OF MALIGNANT NECROPHILIA

Fromm, a practicing psychoanalyst, has devoted long study to the social and political aspects of human motivation. To interpret Hitler he utilizes his gifts for systematic analysis and synthesis and pulls together into one inherently intelligible portrait seemingly disparate aspects of Hitler's character, childhood development, family situation, and social environment (1973). Further, in addition to using the available literature on Hitler and National Socialism, Fromm benefits from lengthy personal contacts with

Speer, Hitler's one-time Minister for War Production and near-confidant.

Like other psychoanalytic interpreters, Fromm reviews the hard core of findings on Hitler, and finds it minimally revealing. His survey of Hitler's parents particularly leaves him —seemingly—puzzled. Much like the historian Smith (on whom he strongly relies), Fromm ponders: "How can we explain that these two well-meaning, stable, very normal, and certainly not destructive people gave birth to the future 'monster,' Adolf Hitler?"[30]

The puzzle deepens when Fromm looks at Adolf's first six—and, according to psychoanalytic theory, most formative—years. During this period Adolf seems to have enjoyed his mother's undisturbed care and attention, suffering no major trauma, with the possible exceptions of the birth of a brother when he was five, and the family's move to Passau for one year: events that occurred at about the same time. Fromm minimizes the possible trauma inherent in these events: "Contrary to the cliché, the evidence shows that instead of suffering pangs of jealousy, young Hitler fully enjoyed the year after his brother's birth."[31] On the family's move to Passau, Fromm quotes Smith, according to whom Hitler enjoyed at Passau "a five-year-old's paradise, playing games and roughhousing with the children of the neighborhood. Miniature wars and fights between cowboys and Indians appear to have been his favorites, and they were to continue as his major diversion for many years."[32]

To solve the puzzle and to account for Hitler's transformation into "monster," Fromm, too, focuses on Hitler's preoedipal vicissitudes, specifically his well-documented overindulgence and overprotection by his mother. But rather than emphasizing any one of the three aspects mentioned earlier—the oral gratification, the primitive conflict, or the nurturant symbiosis—he introduces a still different point of view, one that ties Adolf's overindulgence and overprotection by Klara to his development of a coldly narcissistic, alienated, and totally destructive character.

To explain such character development, Fromm offers the hypothesis of an early "malignant incestuousness" with his mother:

> This hypothesis would lead to the assumption that Hitler's fixation to his mother was not a warm and affectionate one up to age five; that he remained cold and did not break through his narcissistic shell; that she did not assume the role of a real person for him, but that of a symbol for the

impersonal power of earth, fate—and death. If this was so, one could understand why the birth of a brother would not have been the cause for his withdrawal from mother. In fact, one could not even say that he withdrew from her, if it is true that affectively he had never felt close to her . . . . This hypothesis would also explain why Hitler later never fell in love with motherly figures, why the tie to his real mother as a person was replaced by that to blood, soil, the race, and eventually to chaos and death.[33]

For according to Fromm: "The person tied to mother by malignant incestuous bonds remains narcissistic, cold, unresponsive; he is drawn to her as iron is drawn to a magnet; she is the ocean in which he wants to drown; the ground in which he wants to be buried."[34] This line of reasoning leads Fromm to expound Hitler as a clinical case of necrophilia, i.e., of a malignantly destructive person whose whole life's thrust aims at humiliating, killing, maiming, and destroying all that comes within his reach.

Guided by this central hypothesis, Fromm presents his evidence methodically. Hitler, he writes, revealed essential traits of his narcissistic character even at the age of six—among them an inordinate craving for freedom which for Hitler meant, as Fromm notes, "irresponsibility, lack of constraint, and most importantly, 'freedom from reality' . . . . "[35] Not bound to people by ordinary bonds of loyalty and love, he had developed even then a "defective realism," a grandiose belief in his skill and power to control and manipulate others.

As an adolescent, Hitler showed hate and contempt for school because he grandiosely expected to "succeed without trying." Hence any realistic demands enraged him, causing him to escape to the world of games where he could lead and control others, or to indulge in fantasies of becoming a superb artist. While his mother covertly nourished such escapism and retreat into fantasy, his father proved too weak to enforce discipline or a realistic appraisal of societal demands.

This pattern, according to Fromm, continued during Adolf's years in Vienna. But even though he suffered defeat after defeat there, he emerged toughened, his narcissism unbroken, as ". . . everything depended now on wiping out the humiliation by taking revenge on all his 'enemies' and devoting his life to the goal of proving that his narcissistic self-image had not been a phantasy but was reality."[36] He skidded from failure to failure, each failure causing a graver narcissistic wound, a deeper humiliation, than the previous one, yet also a more deadly resolve for revenge.

Drawing on the evidence available at the time he wrote his book, Fromm takes Hitler's attitude toward his mother's death as further evidence of his gross narcissism, stressing that he did not even care to travel to Linz to see his mother in her final hours. For Fromm this is further proof "that Hitler's mother never became to him a person to whom he was lovingly or tenderly attached. She was a symbol of the protecting and admiring goddesses, but also of the goddess of death and chaos. At the same time, she was an object for his sadistic control, arousing a deep fury in him when she was not obliging."[3][7] (As I shall show shortly, we need to re-evaluate Fromm's evidence on this issue in the light of the findings recently reported by Binion.)

Shortly after World War I, Hitler started his career as a leader of men, and increasingly assumed power—despite repeated reversals. This, according to Fromm, marks the turning point at which his passion for destruction—i.e., his necrophilia—could enact in deeds what thus far had remained fantasy. Fromm traces in detail the development and many manifestations of this overriding, irrational passion. He points to Hitler's mania for destroying buildings and cities, amply attested by Speer (1970) and others; to his "scorched earth" decree for Germany in September 1944; and to his plans for the future of the Poles after his victory over them. Fromm quotes H. Picker (1965): "They [the Poles] were to be culturally castrated; teaching was to be restricted to knowledge of traffic signals, some German, and, as to geography, the fact that Berlin is the capital of Germany; arithmetic was entirely superfluous. There was to be no medical care; low living standards; all they were good for was as cheap labor and slaves."[3][8] We are also reminded that Hitler indulged in fantasies of unlimited destruction when he pondered his crushing of anticipated mutinies. He asserted, for example, that faced with a mutiny such as took place in 1918, "He would immediately kill all leaders of opposing political currents, also those of political catholicism, and all inmates of concentration camps. He figured that in this way he would kill several hundred thousand people"[3][9]—a quantity that would have added only negligibly to the number of Jews he actually killed. Not surprisingly, Hitler expected Eva Braun and all the others who followed him loyally to the end to die without question. And as early as January 1942—over a year before Stalingrad—Hitler reveled in fantasies of seeing the German people destroyed. In brief, while ". . . it is correct to say that Hitler was a Jew-hater . . . it is equally correct to say that he was a German-hater. He was a hater of mankind, a hater of life itself."[4][0]

To be sure, Fromm also notes features in Hitler that do not

easily fit a coldly narcissistic and necrophiliac character. For example, he registers Hitler's guilt and near suicide after the death by her own hand of his half-niece and mistress, "Geli" Raubal, in 1931. Fromm also observes that Hitler was never present at a murder or an execution. And when some of his comrades were killed in an attempted coup in Munich (November 9, 1923), he struggled with ideas of suicide and suffered twitchings in his left arm, which returned after the defeat at Stalingrad. Further, he apparently could not tolerate the sight of dead and wounded soldiers. To Fromm, this behavior does not reflect a lack of physical courage (possession of which Hitler amply demonstrated in the First World War) or tender feelings for the German soldiers. Rather, it reflects a phobic or otherwise defensive reaction against the awareness of his destructiveness. Fromm sees this phobic defense as akin to Hitler's overcleanliness, mentioned by Speer, which at times grew into a full-fledged washing compulsion. In sum, Fromm finds that whatever at first sight seems to contradict his portrait of Hitler's necrophiliac destructiveness, on closer inspection reflects either repression, a veneer, simple deceit, or a mixture of the three—thus confirming rather than negating his view of Hitler's basic necrophilia.

Like most other commentators on Hitler, Fromm acknowledges Hitler's various gifts and talents. For example, he notes his capacity to influence, impress, and persuade people, his striking gift for imparting to others his oversimplifications of complex issues, his talent as an actor, including his complete control over his voice, and his ability to terrorize as well as arouse people by his attacks of anger. Further, he refers to Hitler's extraordinary memory, which allowed him to bluff even sophisticated experts, and he takes account of an iron determination and a perseverance even under adversity (amazing in a one-time loafer) that enabled Hitler to delay the final defeat several years after Stalingrad (when the war was actually lost). But Fromm also notes serious defects, particularly in Hitler's sense of reality. These defects speeded his downfall, as they caused him to blunder tactically and strategically. Toward the end his defective reality sense had the taint of delusion. While Russian troops were pushing the fighting nearer and nearer the *Reichskanzlei-Bunker*, Hitler was still commanding nonexisting armies,[41] trying to arouse nonexistent passions, or ordering gruesome, yet no longer executable, punishments for traitors. Yet even in his last days, as a physically and mentally broken man, he remained controlled, according to Fromm.[42] And up to his last living moment he remained the insatiable hater without compassion or pity, the extreme narcissist who, in his final will, apparently without a pang of guilt, advised his fellow Germans not to relent in destroying the Jews and other enemies, while at the same time he implicitly blamed them—the Germans—for not proving themselves worthy of his own leadership.

In drawing his final conclusions, Fromm asserts that ". . . often the intensely destructive person will show a front of kindliness; courtesy; love of family, of children, of animals; he will speak of his ideals and good intentions,"[4][3] thereby deceiving others. To counter such deceit, we must analyze him objectively and without passion in his total human and sociopolitical context, as Fromm set out to do.

From Fromm's analysis of Hitler, geared almost totally to explaining his destructiveness, we turn, next, to the third major perspective offered thus far—that of R. Binion.

BINION'S PERSPECTIVE:
HITLER AS HIS MOTHER'S AVENGER

Binion is a psychohistorian versed in psychoanalytic principles and insights, as his thorough and scholarly work on Lou Andreas-Salomé attests. As with *Frau Lou* (1968), he researched Hitler's personality and background anew and ingeniously (1973). As a result, he arrived at startling and original findings that have yet to find their way into standard biographies. But Binion not only succeeded as an historical researcher; he also integrated his and others' findings into a new, encompassing perspective on Hitler which, above all else, makes inherently intelligible the two main thrusts in Hitler's life: his deadly campaign against the Jews, and his quest for *Lebensraum* in the East. At this writing, only a part of his findings, ideas, and sources has been published, and his book on Hitler and Germany is still forthcoming. Nonetheless, what is already on record alters and deepens our understanding of Hitler and, among other things, helps us to assess Fromm's thesis. In the following summary of Binion's position, I risk massive oversimplification and omit his complex and detailed documentation of sources, to which the reader is referred.

Binion, like Fromm and others, builds his case on Hitler's early close—if you wish, preoedipal—relationship with Klara. But he emphasizes facts that Fromm underemphasized or ignored. The first of these, already mentioned, is that young Klara, after her marriage to Alois, gave birth to three children in close succession, all of whom died in early childhood within weeks after the third birth. Young Otto, we saw, lived only three days, and Gustav and Ida were buried soon afterward.[44] Here Binion focuses on the trauma that Klara suffered due to this triple loss. Twenty years later, Adolf's boyhood friend, Kubizek, so Binion reminds us, observed in Klara " 'the muted sorrow that . . . spoke out of her features' and that, as Kubizek discovered, was due to the 'fearful trials' of her young motherhood. 'Whenever I saw her,' Kubizek later recollected, 'I felt . . . compassion and the need to do something for her.' "[45]

Adolf Hitler was conceived some six months after these tragic deaths. Edmund, the next child, was born almost four years later; Binion theorizes that the intervening period of infertility was not accidental. Rather, Klara "*re*lived her traumatic maternal experience (from first conception to third death) by not having—suppressing—the three children involved."[46] He adduces several arguments that make such fertility control plausible, adding that she might have breastfed Hitler inordinately long, thereby helping to keep herself barren. Once Adolf was born, Klara, gripped by her traumatic losses, over-protected and over-indulged Adolf as an infant—and afterwards. Kubizek reports that Klara once told him that "she had lived in continual worry lest she lost him" (i.e., Adolf), "adding that this worry only ended with her death." Therefore, Binion concludes, "Adolf was her compensation for her triple loss; she guarded him as anxiously as she did even while she unconsciously relived her triple loss; *thus he sucked in that maternal trauma with his mother's milk.*"[48]

Hitler, according to Binion—and here he clashes with Fromm—responded to his mother's overanxious and overprotective feeding of him by becoming not a ruthless narcissist but an anxious, worrying, and caring son. To decide whether Binion or Fromm is right here, we must, above all else, know Hitler's reactions to his mother's terminal illness and death. If it is true that Adolf, as Fromm contends, almost forgot the dying Klara while loafing in Vienna, the case of a coldly narcissistic and uncaring Hitler is strengthened; if not, it is weakened. Here Binion presents evidence that contradicts Fromm.

Essentially, Fromm relied here on Smith's evaluation of the available evidence. This left no doubt that Hitler went to Vienna in late September, or perhaps early October, of 1907 (as he had to take his examination at the Academy of Fine Arts, which was held only once a year). However, there was conflicting testimony as to whether Hitler returned to Linz by December 21, i.e., before the date of his mother's death. Kubizek and Bloch assert that he did, but Jetzinger said otherwise. To support his claim, Jetzinger

(1956) underscored Kubizek's and Bloch's unreliability on details, and introduced a (in his opinion) more reliable witness—a postmaster's widow alleged to have known the Hitlers. Her account, also given many years after the event and tailored for Nazi audiences, failed to mention that Hitler arrived in time before Klara's death. In weighing the evidence, Smith felt that Kubizek and Bloch had strong reasons to push the creation of the "monster Hitler" off to later times and onto other "companions" and therefore to cultivate the image of a loving Adolf caring for his dying mother. Consequently, Smith accepted Jetzinger's version of events, which thus also become that of Fromm.

More recently, though, Smith changed his mind. He admits that: "Now Rudolph Binion presents two pieces of strong evidence that tip the other way. The first is the statement by Paula Hitler from the John Toland collection that Adolf was there through the whole period. The second is Binion's truly splendid decipherment of Dr. Bloch's medical record . . . which seems to me to establish that Adolf was in Linz at least part of the time during Klara's final illness."[49] Even though Smith subsequently qualifies the inferences he draws from Dr. Bloch's records, he finds that "the evidence now tips in favor of the conclusion that Hitler was probably in Linz when his mother died."[50] Thus, Binion found that Adolf, far from putting his dying mother out of his mind, lived with her as much as he could, agonized over her suffering, and nursed her tenderly day and night in her last weeks. Rather than an anxious mother trying to save her threatened child, we find the child, grown into adolescent, trying to save his sick and threatened mother.

Against this background of a reversed nursing situation, Binion re-interprets Hitler's major motivational dynamics. While this interpretation builds on Binion's own data, it also incorporates the ideas of others, particularly those of Kurth as developed in her study "The Jew and Adolf Hitler" (1947).

Central to Binion's theory is the role of Dr. Eduard Bloch, his mother's Jewish doctor. It was he, we saw, who in January 1907 diagnosed her chest pain as due to breast cancer and who at once had one breast removed. Subsequently, under increasing pressure from Hitler to do something—anything—he undertook an intensive, expensive local treatment with iodoform. It ended with the patient's death some seven weeks later. The death was slow, painful, and torturous. Hitler overtly revered Dr. Bloch, who was then popular as a dedicated *Arme Leute Doktor* (a poor people's doctor). At the same time, he pressured him into drastic actions —taken, so it seems, only guiltily and reluctantly by Bloch—which finally poisoned his mother—and also turned out to be exorbitantly expensive. Throughout his adult years, Hitler continued to idealize Bloch. He sent him several appreciative postcards and as late as 1940 allowed him to emigrate to the United States and escape the holocaust. But covertly and unconsciously he blamed him, in helpless, retaliatory fury, as his mother's poisoner and an unscrupulous profiteer. This fury broke loose approximately eleven years later when Hitler, temporarily blinded by poison gas and hospitalized in Pasewalk, suffered the shock of Germany's overthrow. He then hallucinated a summons from on high to reverse Germany's defeat. At this point his political career began. Growing increasingly radical in his actions, he turned his wrath against the Jews, denouncing them as parasites, profiteers, and poisoners of Germany—a Germany that, as "motherland," was now taking the place of his mother. When Hitler, in 1941, personally ordered the final removal of the Jews through poison gas, he spoke of "removing, extirpating, excising the Jewish cancer from the national flesh," thus using "the very language of his mother's operation of January 1907."[5 1] Thus he belatedly likened "cure and punishment"—now to be inflicted on six million Jews—to the original events.

While removing the Jews, Hitler also conquered *Lebensraum* in the East and thereby promised to wipe out a German national trauma dating back to the final weeks of World War I, when Germany's conquests vanished and her inflated expectations were extinguished. His personal experience of shock and sudden deprivation, suffered by a once overindulged and ever greedy child and revived at the end of World War I, now resonated with that of the German people who, along with him, had found themselves deprived and betrayed. In tuning himself to "the inner will of the nation," Hitler invited the Germans to master their collective trauma by repeating it—i.e., by undertaking a new war—much as his own mother had tried to master the triple loss of her children by recreating it through her (according to Binion, unconsciously willed) infertility. Hitler's ruthless Eastern campaign served his two main goals, as it conquered Russia's expanses and at the same time destroyed the centers of European Jewry.

In summary, Binion illuminates the psychological determinants of what he (along with many leading Hitler scholars)[5 2] views as the two major thrusts in Hitler's political life: his deadly hatred of Jews, and his quest for *Lebensraum*. In so doing, Binion widens, modifies, and sharpens the earlier psychoanalytic perspectives on Hitler. He attaches new meaning to Hitler's preoedipal vicissitudes

and also accommodates—within limits—the classical oedipal
formula. The wrath Hitler directed at Jews and other "enemies" of
Germany now links up with the wrath he felt (but dissociated)
vis-à-vis the Jewish Dr. Bloch, the "profiteer" and "poisoner" of
his mother, and from there—possibly—with the wrath that his
"castrating" father had aroused, a wrath which now found a
substitute target in Dr. Bloch. At the same time, Binion gives new
significance to Hitler's early close bond with Klara. In asserting
that Germany later took his mother's place, he raises questions, as
yet largely unanswered, as to how this bond replaced the original
one and how the wills of Hitler and Germany meshed. These
questions concern, above all, the group processes which operated
at that time. We shall turn to them in Chapter V.

But while Binion reconciled some of the earlier psychoanalytic
findings and viewpoints concerning Hitler, he challenged others,
among which those of Fromm stand out. For even though Fromm
and Binion seem to take off from the same base—Hitler's early
indulgence by, and closeness to, his mother—their conclusions
diverge. Fromm, we saw, sees here a "malignant incestuousness"
which subsequently resulted in a totally unrelated, coldly
narcissistic human being—one who, in the words of Hitler's
popular biographer R. Payne, " . . . had no loyalties, no religious
faith, no culture, no family ties . . ." whose ". . . strength lay in
the fact that he was totally alienated," and to whom "it was all
one . . . whether he conquered the world or shot himself in the
mouth."[53] For Binion, in contrast, this early experience of
mutuality lay at the root of a relatedness and loyalty so deep,
albeit twisted, that it consumed Hitler's life in efforts to do repairs
and execute heinous revenge.

It is this clash of interpretations—with their differing
implications for how we view human aggression and
destructiveness, how we understand individual, group, and family
dynamics, and how we assign accountability—that has shaped the
queries and thoughts that follow. To find answers, I shall draw
chiefly on my work with separating parents and children, as
elsewhere reported (1973a, 1973e, 1974c), and on the resulting
theoretical formulations. With this objective in mind, we return to
Hitler's adolescence.

CHAPTER II

HITLER BOUND AND DELEGATED BY HIS MOTHER

HITLER: REBELLIOUS OR COMPLIANT?

Among the many puzzling events in Hitler's life, those of his adolescence stand out. I refer to his unexpected failure at the *Realschule*, his undisciplined ways, his inability to concentrate, his rageful outbursts, his—seeming or real—emotional and intellectual retardation, his parasitic existence at home and later in Vienna. Hitler himself evokes here the spectre of a defiant, rebellious youth who, bent on becoming an artist, resists all parental efforts—be these well- or ill-meaning—to mold him into something he refuses to be. Many scholarly as well as non-scholarly biographers have since subscribed to the notion of Adolf's "rebellious adolescence."

Yet here—and this introduces my own perspective—I must disagree. For, in my years of work with adolescents and their families, I have come to revise my notions of adolescent "rebellion." Here my experience as therapist of whole families has been especially important. At the outset of joint family meetings, I have been told again and again that this or that adolescent was the most "rebellious" family member, also the most uncontrollable, most bent on mischief, most deeply into drugs, most hell-bent on disrupting classwork and on failing in school.

But the more I saw of these young "rebels" and their parents, the more I doubted their rebelliousness. On the contrary: rather than seeing them as the most self-determined and most defiant within the family, I came to see them as the most compliant. I realized that in their very rebelliousness they complied with their parents' deeper expectations and wishes, albeit in frequently conflicting and confusing ways. Consequently, I came to view them as "delegates of their parents" (1972a, 1973d, 1974c).

To make clear what this implies, I must now take the reader approximately 1000 years back in time to an era that has always fascinated me—that of early medieval Europe. For this happens to be the period in history that inspired me to conceive of *the adolescent as delegate of his parents* (1973d), as it is this period which created a relationship that served as my paradigm: the relationship between feudal lord and vassal.

ON THE SOURCES OF FIDELITY AND LOYALTY

This relationship had as its psychological and moral core an intense bond of loyalty. An extant letter that a Frankish noblewoman by the name of Dhuoda wrote to her son William, in 843 A.D., advising him on his new obligations as vassal to King Charles the Bald, offers a glimpse of this bond:

Since God, as I believe, and your father Bernard have chosen you, in the flower of your youth, to serve Charles as your lord, I urge you ever to remember the record of your family, illustrious on both sides, and not to serve your master simply to satisfy him outwardly, *but to maintain toward him and his service in all things a devoted and unwavering fealty both of body and soul.*[1]

The word "fealty," as used in this letter, derives from the Latin noun *fidelitas*, in English "fidelity," which Erikson (1968) recently used to define a crucial feature and need of adolescence. Such an idea of fidelity governed the conduct of both parties in the lord-vassal relationship, showing itself in the ways each partner fulfilled specific rights and obligations. For example:

The vassal was to respect the lord, promote his interests, attend him in his manor or castle, give him counsel on request, aid him financially in special cases, house him during his periodic visits to the fief, and fight at his command for about forty days a year. In return, the lord was to treat his vassal as an honorable subordinate, assist him in emergency situations, and seek justice in his behalf.[2]

For a long time, these specific rights and obligations appeared anchored in an unquestioned social order, which was held to be unchanging—the order of early feudal Europe. But the decades before the year 1000 A.D. were times of change. Then, as now, commerce and communication increased, populations grew, urban centers developed, and communal ties were strained. At the same time, new professional careers, new life styles, and new values emerged, while existing hierarchies and authorities were questioned. All these developments affected the loyalty bond between lord and vassal.

The impact upon it was not clear-cut, however. Though the loyalty bond lost some of its anchorage in the social order and thus loosened up, at the same time it became more complex and significant. For the need to remain loyal combined now with a need for action (or, if you wish, adventure) which propelled the vassal out of his lord's orbit, thus highlighting as well as straining the bond. And it was at this point that the vassal turned more and more into his lord's *delegate*, as I came to define the term.

THE MEANING OF DELEGATE

What, then, do I mean by *delegate?* As I wrote elsewhere (1972a), the Latin verb *delegare* has two main meanings. It means, first, to send out and, second, to entrust with a mission. The latter meaning implies that the delegate, although sent out, remains beholden to the sender, as the vassal remained beholden to the lord. Thus, where a child serves as a delegate of his parents, he is allowed and encouraged to move out of the parental orbit—up to a point! He is held on a long leash of loyalty, as it were, and his sending out is qualified. His loyalty must not be too blind, tight, and restrictive, though; rather, it must allow for initiative, relative autonomy, selectivity, and differentiation. Otherwise, the delegate could not fulfill missions that demand ingenuity and skill.

Such a delegate tries to sustain or recoup his parents' (or lord's) approbation and love, a love now made contingent on how he executes his mission(s). The more difficult and risky the mission, the more he shows his fidelity, and thus the more he can expect to sustain or recoup his sender's love.

To serve as a faithful delegate-vassal remains (relatively) easy as long as missions appear clearly defined and anchored in an unquestioned social and family order; it becomes difficult and problematical when missions change in the wake of wider social change, and when they are shrouded in ambiguity.

To make clearer what is involved, let me once more go back a thousand years or so and consider a phenomenon—the Crusades—which deeply affected the order of medieval Europe and which is relevant to my chosen theme.

In 1095, Pope Urban II exhorted all men of Christian faith to free the shrines of the Holy Land from the infidels. Thereby he tapped, it seems, fervent loyalties which feudal Europe had bred, but which social changes had pried loose from the old lord-vassal relationship, and lifted them to a higher plane on which God himself (or his representative on earth) became Lord. As God's delegates, the Christian crusaders thirsted to execute missions *ad majorem Dei gloriam*, deeming no sacrifice too large. But also—and here enters the ambiguity—all too often they seemed to alloy lofty intent with questionable motives. Thus, while papal dispensation guaranteed them their souls' salvation—i.e., God's everlasting love and approbation—they often, historians noted, "put mundane ambitions ahead of spiritual redemption." Inevitably, the question arose whether they were faithful delegates of the Lord, or whether they merely craved fame, booty, new estates, and an escape from the humdrum of everyday life. In brief, it was no longer clear whether they remained God's delegates or whether they were pursuing their own goals, more or less selfishly and hence autonomously. Let us, keeping in mind this ambiguity, return to the world of modern adolescence, and assess its bearing on Hitler.

This world was and is subject to changes even deeper and more rapid than those of a thousand years ago. Here I want to focus, above all, on changes in today's Western family and specifically on the relations between generations. Among these changes I count most important the growing ambiguity as to what the two parties—parents and children—need, and should expect, from each other. In earlier, less changeful, and less complex times, the two parties found little cause for question and bewilderment. Their mutual needs, rights, and obligations seemed more or less self-evident. Parents provided children with food, shelter, and care. They prepared them for survival in society by transmitting skills and strengthening the sense of self-worth; possibly also by securing their careers with the help of money or a distinguished name. Children, in turn, were expected to honor their parents, to add to the family's sustenance (e.g., by working as farm hands), and to support their parents in old age. Such a balance of specific needs, rights, and obligations was not unlike the one we found in the bond between lord and vassal, and in a similar way became more intricate and more ambiguous, at the same time more important, as our Western world changed.

For example, Western parents—particularly those of the well-to-do middle-class—came less and less to need their children's material help, in contrast to what we still find in underdeveloped (and mainly rural) societies. And Western children, for their part, have become less and less able to give such help—even if they so wished. By requiring the young to protract their educations in the quest for advancement and skills, or to compete harder in the shrinking job-market for the unskilled, an industrial/technological society effectively prevents them from serving as props and bastions to their elders.

Further: Western parents seem less and less equipped to prepare their children for life in a rapidly changing world. Many parents today, for example, are too set in their ways and therefore unable to gauge the implications of expanding birth rates, of ecological devastation, of global nuclear war, and hence cannot envision, much less provide, the tools—the habits of thought, the skills, the expertise—their children will need to master this threatened world in which they (the children, not their parents) must live. Hence the children cannot help becoming, or at least appearing, precociously questioning and assertive. At the same time they find themselves, for increasingly long periods of time, financially dependent on their elders and their institutions (such as welfare agencies or college administrations). And while much seems to have changed here since Hitler's adolescence, the basic constellation has not.

Finally—and this signifies perhaps the most important shift in the balance of intergenerational needs, rights, and obligations—while parents less and less need their children's *economic* contribution, they more and more need, it appears to me, their *psychological* help. And the children, as loyal delegates, can be expected to try to meet just that need and to insure their parents' psychological, rather than material, survival.

But like the medieval vassal who turned crusader, an adolescent who becomes his parents' delegate operates in a complex and ambiguous field. For one thing, his missions are now often covertly and ambiguously entrusted and therefore elusive; for another, these missions often appear at odds with his own need—which we may call *the* need of adolescence—to become his own person, to live his own life, and to pursue his own ends. To chart this complex scenario, which defies any simple formula about the conflict of generations, let us look more closely at the sorts of missions that modern parents entrust to their adolescents.

THE DELEGATE'S MISSIONS

The psychoanalytic constructs of id, ego, and superego provide a framework for orientation here, since they permit us to distinguish between missions whose primary service is (respectively) to the parental id, ego, or superego.

Where we deal with id-level missions, the delegate provides a parent with id-nutriment that the parent, for one reason or another, cannot obtain for himself and therefore must enjoy by proxy. Here the child stimulates the parent's imagination with hints or vivid descriptions of his exploits, allowing his parent to experience vicarious thrills. The latter, while seeking such thrills, may also conveniently disown them, as when he scolds and punishes the child for the very things he (more or less covertly) has asked him to do. The thrills can be primarily sexual. Here the parent may covertly goad the delegate to engage in sexual activities, including perversions and orgies, on which the parent wants to "feed." Or the thrills may have a more oral, pregenital flavor, as when the parent covertly instigates and vicariously enjoys his child's drug and drinking parties. In other cases, the basis for the thrills may lie in a desire to do the forbidden and to defy authority. In such cases a parent may covertly encourage and enjoy his child's delinquent and rebellious behavior.

Where a child's service is primarily to his parent's ego, he boosts the latter's hold on reality. This he can do in various ways. Like the medieval vassal who defended and extended his lord's power over things and people, he can defend and extend his parent's power base, i.e., fight his parent's battles. Or he might—a rather common mission—seek experiences and information about the world which the parent, for one reason or another, cannot seek himself. Thus, among runaway adolescents whom I studied intensively, I found not only thrill-providing but also information-providing delegates. For example, one adventurous runaway girl, on whom I have reported elsewhere (1972a, 1973a), gave her father an object lesson on how one could move into new environments, live on little money, and cope with unfamiliar conflicts and situations. Her father, we discovered, was a runaway manqué: at one time during the period of almost two years that I worked with this family he advertised his house for sale; at another he made a hasty trip to a big Midwestern city, supposedly to start a new business, though in fact he merely loitered about. Typically, all his attempts to run away and make new starts fizzled, as he was too restricted and too afraid. Therefore he recruited (again covertly) his runaway daughter as his "scout," to borrow a term from D. Reiss,[3] yet at the same time disowned his need for her "scout services."

We may also speak of ego-type missions in cases where the delegate serves to maintain his parent's defensive organization, i.e., serves to protect and support his parent's fragile ego by sparing the latter heightened conflict and ambivalence. As these ego-type conflicts invariably involve the superego (which, according to Freud, is part of the ego), I shall describe them now under that rubric.

Freud (1933) came to distinguish three main functions of the superego: to serve as ego-ideal, to self-observe, and to act as conscience. Any of these three functions—relating, of course, to the *parent's* superego—can stake out a delegate's major mission.

Where the delegate principally serves his parent's ego-ideal, he is sent out into life to realize unfulfilled parental aspirations. Here the parent expects the adolescent to become the actor, scientist, physician, or financial tycoon that the parent himself failed to become.

If his main mission is to serve his parent's self-observation and self-confirmation, the adolescent may be delegated to provide a living contrast by being bad. He is to be mischief-maker, troubled, crazy, or delinquent. His function here is similar to that of "inferior" Southern Negroes whose white masters boosted their own inwardly doubted "superiority" by constantly observing and confirming the Negroes' "inferiority."

Finally, a delegate may chiefly have to alleviate his parent's excessively strict conscience. In this situation parents covertly encourage an adolescent to commit, and seek punishment for, delinquent acts about which they themselves still harbor (mostly unconscious) guilt. Here we may speak of "superego lucunae"—i.e., deficiencies in a person's moral orientation and supporting psychic structures—which Johnson and Szurek (1952) linked to the methods by which parents unconsciously initiate and foster antisocial behavior in their children. The delegate's delinquency in such cases mirrors parental superego lacunae but also serves to blot them out, as he turns into an unwitting perpetrator of mischief and receiver of punishment. Here we find adolescents who start to steal in the same manner and about the same time as their fathers did before them. Such a father can now comfortably tell himself that his own adolescent stealing could not have been so bad after all, as it is obviously an adolescent thing to do. Whatever residual guilt was left in the father is expiated by proxy, as he prompts his son to further punishment-seeking. Other delegates appear recruited mainly as their parents' redeemers. Here I am reminded of those German students who labored in Israel's kibbutzim in order to atone for their parents' crimes. These youngsters called their action "sign of atonement" (*Aktion Sühnezeichen*). The parents had apparently succeeded in delegating their children to go to Israel by unloading onto them the pain of guilt and the need for repair work which they themselves were unable to "own."

How do the above phenomena fit into the overall process of adolescent separation and individuation? To examine this question, we must now consider certain vicissitudes to which adolescent delegates are subject. We may speak of the derailments of the delegating process. These involve, first, conflicts of missions and, second, conflicts of loyalties.

CONFLICTS OF MISSIONS AND CONFLICTS OF LOYALTIES

Authors such as A. Freud (1946), E. H. Erikson (1950, 1959), and P. Blos (1962, 1970), have alerted us to the many (mainly intrapsychic) conflicts of the modern adolescent. These conflicts beset his quest for autonomy and identity. They arise as his aggressive and libidinal drives intensify, his defensive organization realigns, and his relational vicissitudes increase. Conflicts of missions and conflicts of loyalties, as here intended, superimpose themselves on, or interweave with, these well-known conflicts. Such an added conflict load can easily exhaust or even break an adolescent.

Elsewhere (1972a) I described a young girl in the grip of conflicting missions entrusted to her by both parents. Her father, a frustrated high school dropout, wanted an instant academic success, a house-bound, caring companion, and an erotic playmate, as well as a thrill-providing delegate, all in one package; her mother, an obese and—in her own eyes—ugly woman, expected a glamorous, but also a demure and virtuous, maiden. The girl loyally tried to fulfill these many conflicting missions, but, unable to do so, broke down and had to be hospitalized.

T. Lidz and his associates (1973), and recently I. Boszormenyi-Nagy and G. Spark (1973), have described various conflicts of loyalties. Here a (frequently schizophrenic) child, as delegate and ally of one parent, is pitted against the other parent. The child's mission in such situations demands that he devalue, expose, ridicule—in brief, destroy—this other parent. The resulting conflicts can be unbearably intense and guilt-laden as Hamlet (among others) has shown.

OTHER DERAILMENTS OF THE DELEGATING PROCESS

While conflicts of missions and loyalties overburden the adolescent, other vicissitudes pervert or even cancel his status as delegate. The Latin word *delegare*, we saw, means, first, to send out and, second, to entrust with a mission. These two meanings stake out two possible conditions under which delegates cease to be delegates—when they have missions, but are not sent out; or when they are sent out, but have no missions. We deal, then, with extremes which, albeit in opposite ways, derail the delegating process. Both make for a pathological separation of adolescence.

In the first extreme—where the delegate has missions but is not sent out—he stays tied to his parents' orbit. We may speak here of overburdened and bound adolescents. Psychologically, such adolescents may have to remain babies whom their parents can always indulge and infantilize. Or they may have to serve their parents' unending self-observation in ways that maximally jeopardize the children's own growth. I think here of adolescents who, to an unusual extent, must embody and externalize the badness and craziness that a parent, in his innermost self, feels and fears to be his personal fate because such madness looms as part of the whole family's endowment. Living under the (disavowed) threat and spell of madness, such a parent often seems impelled to search for—and, in this process, induce—madness in the child. Thus, the child becomes the external caretaker of the parent's extended madness, and for this reason can never be allowed out of the latter's psychological sight.

It is not only such extreme missions that keep a delegate parent-bound. In addition, an extreme type of parent-child transaction usually comes into play. Elsewhere I called this the *binding* mode (1972a, 1974c) in contrast to other transactional modes, which I named the *delegating* and the *expelling* modes. These modes operate as the covert organizing background to the more overt and specific child-parent (or therapist-patient) interactions (1972d).[4] From the vantage point here chosen, the binding mode represents one extreme vicissitude which negates the delegating process. For parents interact (or transact) here with the child in ways that seem designed to keep the latter totally tied to the parental orbit and locked in the family ghetto, i.e., prevent his being sent out. Such binding, I showed, can occur on three major levels.

First, a child can become bound primarily by the exploitation of his dependency needs: he is offered undue regressive gratification, and we are inclined to speak of id-binding.

Second, binding can operate on a more cognitive level. Here the parent interferes with his child's differentiated self-awareness and self-determination by mystifying the child about what he feels, needs, and wants. He misdefines the child to himself, as it were. G. Bateson (1969) and, with his associates (1956, 1963); H. Bruch (1962); H. Searles (1959); L. C. Wynne (1963a, 1963b) and M. T. Singer (1965a, 1965b); T. Lidz and his associates (1965); J. Haley (1959); and R. D. Laing (1965), among others, have illuminated various features of this interactional process. It often feeds on idiosyncratic language and idiosyncratic patterns of communication. We can call cognitive binding ego-binding, as the binder forces the bindee to rely on the binder's distorted and distorting ego instead of developing and using his own discriminating ego.

Binding can operate, finally, on a third level where the child's loyalty, rather than being compatible with initiative and selectivity, remains undifferentiated and archaic, albeit formidably intense. Children who are bound chiefly on this level are likely to experience any thought of, not to mention attempt at, separation as the number one crime for which only the harshest punishment will do. These children, whom we may call superego-bound, are prone to suffer maximal primitive breakaway guilt that often operates unconsciously and gives rise to acts either of massive self-destruction or of heroic atonement. A longitudinal study of adolescents of high risk for schizophrenia and their families, conducted over a period of six years at the National Institute of Mental Health, allowed me to examine such archaic loyalty-boundness in depth. For example, I followed two youngsters, both of them diagnosed as schizophrenic, who courted death at a time when they most seriously seemed to be breaking away from their parents. Both became runaways but, typically, had no peers to run to, only their idiosyncratic introjects to follow. I therefore spoke of them as lonely schizoid runaways (1973a). They appeared to roam around aimlessly and stumbled into one potentially dangerous situation after the other. One was finally killed when a speeding car ran him over in the sleeping bag which he had placed close to the side of a country road; the other was killed when he waved a knife in the face of a policeman, who shot him instantly. (The policeman was responding to a call for help: the boy had harrassed a number of other people with his knife.) From my knowledge of these schizophrenic adolescents and their families, I had no doubt that their thinly veiled suicides reflected attempts to appease their excruciating breakaway guilt.

Many schizophrenic adolescents appear maximally bound on all three of these levels: id-binding, mystification, and archaic loyalty.

In the other extreme vicissitude, adolescents are sent out, yet have no missions to fulfill. Here their plight is the opposite of the above: instead of being clung to for sheer (parental) survival, they are expendable, as they have little if anything to offer. They are subject to the expelling mode—the opposite of the binding mode—as elsewhere described. Psychologically and economically, these children are family surplus, at best uneasily tolerated, at worst brutally rejected, but always insidiously neglected. Rather than centripetally bound, they appear centrifugally adrift. Many of them turn into wayward youths, unfettered, but also unrestrained by ordinary loyalty, concern, and guilt. The word "wayward," according to Webster's Dictionary, derives from "awayward," which means "turned away,' and suggests expulsion as well as escape. The turned-away person is, again according to Webster's, self-willed, wanton, and prone to follow his or her own caprices. Along with that, he or she appears to obey no clear principle or law and tends therefore to do the opposite of what is desired or expected. Many of these wayward youths we call sociopaths. It is difficult to say which is the worse fate—to be bound and to reel under a "mission impossible," or to be wayward and have no mission at all.

THE NEED TO SERVE AS DELEGATE

The above helps us to consider a central question: are parents entitled to recruit their children as delegates and satisfy their psychological needs through them? My answer is "yes"—up to a point!

Children, I believe, have a need to serve as delegates. In such service they are given direction, a primary identity, a sense of importance, and missions. These, to them, are all vitally needed gifts. However—and this is central—such service must leave room for increasing (relative) autonomy, for shifts in loyalty—away from the parents to peers and alternate adults—and for a constant renegotiation of the generations' mutual needs, rights, and obligations. We may speak of a liberating dialectic that needs to be built into the delegating process.

In cases where this process is derailed, this liberating dialectic cannot unfold. For here parents either burden their child with conflicts of missions or loyalties, bind him excessively with "missions impossible," or leave him footloose and missionless. In each case, they exploit him psychologically because, in each case, they frustrate his needs—such as his need to be loved and to be found important, or to individuate and shape his own destiny—for the sake of their own needs.

A TRANSGENERATIONAL PERSPECTIVE

What compels parents thus to abuse their delegates? To find the answer, we must finally consider the parents' own histories and growths and, most importantly, their relationship to *their* parents. We find, then, for example, that the mother who feeds on her thrill-providing daughter had an adolescence that was joyless and barren. Therefore, she recruits her daughter to make up for what she missed. Or, we find that the father who makes his son serve his (the father's) self-observation and, in the process, binds and implants madness in the boy, labors under a terrible burden: he is haunted by the spectre of mad relatives or ancestors, as Scott and Ashworth (1969) have shown. Hence, he grew up with the notion and expectation, frightening beyond comprehension, that madness again would strike his tainted family. It was in an attempt to control, contain, and neutralize his ever-present fear of madness that he delegated his child to enact it and thereby turned him, unwittingly, into a delegate manqué, i.e., a mad and therefore totally bound family member. Or we find that expelling and neglecting parents—parents who deprive their children of a sense of importance and mission—were denied these gifts by their own parents. They failed to give because they were never given to. In sum, we find that exploiting and neglecting parents were themselves exploited and neglected, and that they recruit these children for overdue repair work, taking them to account for what their own parents did or did not do to them. I. Boszormenyi-Nagy (1972), to whom I here feel deeply indebted, has explored this transgenerational perspective with originality, casting new light on the intergenerational balance of mutual needs, rights, and obligations. This balance, we realize now, frequently disfavors the children because of unsettled accounts that had accrued before they were born.

HITLER'S PARENTS RECONSIDERED

With these perspectives in mind, we return now to Hitler and consider anew his parents and how they related to him. How, we ask, did they recruit him as delegate?

To find an answer, we must recall the times in which his parents lived: the last decades of the Austrian Empire, times beset by social unrest and cultural change, even though there were vestiges of a seemingly unchanging, God-ordained order. The aging Emperor Franz Josef, reigning through half a century, seemed to embody such an order, as did the colossal Baroque buildings in Vienna, the majestic Catholic churches, and the military and administrative hierarchies of the Austrian state. But many forces tore away at that stability. The national minorities that composed the Empire were in ferment and pulled the country apart. In Vienna workers protested and were shot down in rows. Radical slogans and revolutionary ideas swept the country and particularly its capital. These, we must remember, were the times when Nietzsche's thoughts began to take hold of many German-speaking people, and when Hugo von Hoffmansthal, Zweig, Schnitzler, Freud, Kraus, Musil, and many other seminal authors lived and wrote in Vienna.[5] Science and new technologies were expanding, and new industrial and commercial developments were upsetting existing ways of life, bringing new opportunities to some, setbacks to others, and uncertainties to all.

A NEW LOOK AT HITLER'S FATHER

Hitler's father's life exemplifies some of the new opportunities offered by such a time of change. For he rose, we saw, higher than any other Hitler or Hiedler had ever risen. Born into an illiterate environment, he taught himself to read and write, and, starting life as the illegitimate son of a peasant maid, rose to become a respected paterfamilias. Beginning as a shoemaker, he went on to become a senior customs official and advanced from the lower to the middle class, and from poverty to (relative) wealth and land ownership. No wonder Alois presented himself as a proud and domineering man.

It appears, however, that his social rise was not without cost to himself and others. While he was conscientious and hard-working, he was also emotionally unstable, inordinately restless, and perhaps at times mentally disturbed. According to one source, he possibly once entered an asylum.[6] Also, in the opinion of at least one analyst,[7] he combined an overriding determination with a flexible conscience, shown especially in how he manipulated rules and records to his own ends, while maintaining a facade of legitimacy. (For example, in applying for papal approval to marry his legal cousin Klara, he stressed his two small motherless children, needing Klara's care, but failed to mention her pregnancy.)

To assess Alois' possible role as delegate (of *his* parents) and delegator (of Adolf), we need to know about his ties to his own parents. Yet here much remains vague. While it is difficult enough to reconstruct the psychological climate of Adolf's family of origin, it is even more difficult, if not impossible, to do so in that of his parents. We know that Alois' mother, Maria Anna Schicklgruber, was 42—and thus relatively old—when she gave birth to the boy and that thereafter she had only ten more years to live, five of these as the wife of Georg Hiedler, later Alois' "official" father. W. Maser[8] describes her as a shrewd, resilient peasant woman who even amassed a modest fortune. I, for one, suspect that Alois, in rising so high, realized her hidden aspirations and served as *her* delegate, even though she died too early to see him succeed.

But while he possibly fulfilled his mother's dreams, Alois largely failed as father and loyal husband, as he apparently cared little for his children and very likely had constant affairs. He preferred to spend his evenings away from home, either drinking or chatting with his cronies in the local inn, or tending his garden and beehives. According to one informant whom Jetzinger quotes (1956), Alois hardly saw his family at all. It was only after his early retirement, it seems, that he became more aware of his children and, as a result, became more irritated and embroiled with the young Adolf. This pattern is rather common in certain types of "successful" delegates. To fulfill their missions they must pursue them so singlemindedly that they cannot but neglect and exploit their human environment, and most of all their families.

The offshoot of this was that Adolf's neglectful and exploitative father came to exemplify to the boy the advantages of power, dominance, autocratic rule, and possibly manipulative cunning, yet failed to instill in him those warm, admiring feelings which he needed in order to build a secure male identity that could pull him away from a too-binding and over gratifying mother. Alois equally failed to provide a model for men-women relationships that were loyal, tender, respectful, and sexually fulfilling. Moreover, while he was threatening as a dominating figure he was too distant and unempathic to provide true guidance and executive control. Thus, I believe, it was not he, despite his power and superior status, who represented to Adolf the "stronger parent's reality" (Stierlin, 1959), but the weak, submissive, self-effacing Klara, who therefore became Adolf's main delegator.

KLARA AS ADOLF'S DELEGATOR

Klara was the seventh of eleven children. The little we know of her family suggests that she was not fortunate. Her peasant parents and siblings were poor, and sometimes in desperate straits, so that Klara grew up amidst fierce competition for scarce material—and, we may assume, emotional—resources. It was probably in an attempt to escape the strains and misery at home that, when barely fifteen years old, she sought respite in the relatively affluent home of her "uncle, Alois"—even though this meant she had to serve as his lowly maid.

In stark contrast to Alois, she seemed ill-equipped to use the opportunities that the changing times offered. As a simple-minded, uneducated, unassuming peasant girl, she was one of those persons who, in the words of Bertolt Brecht, were destined to "walk in darkness." For, according to Brecht:

There are those who walk in darkness,
There are those who walk in light,
We can see the latter only
For the rest are out of sight.

Denn die einen gehn in Dunkel,
Und die andern gehn im Licht,
Doch man sieht nur die im Lichte,
Die im Dunkel sieht man nicht.[9]

And in contrast to Alois—who to some extent dared to defy established authorities, as when he lambasted and ridiculed "black clericals"—she had to hold back, if not deny, her feelings of rage and frustration and seems to have revered in childlike piety the Catholic church and its representatives. Without doubt, she internalized the church's simple notions of what constituted sin and what aroused guilt and shame.

Given her low and captive status, nearly everything that Klara could want from life had to come to her through her husband or children. But with her husband her leverage was minimal. Throughout her married life, we saw, she related to Alois from a confusing and helpless position. But further, she had, according to Smith,

> ... few close connections with other people and the few she had were mainly with family members. In her day-to-day affairs, only the Church gave her an approved activity extending beyond the narrow confines of her home. Alois insisted she attend regularly as an expression of his belief that the woman's place was in the kitchen and in the church. There was no religious conviction in Alois' idea, nor did social pressures play a part; only duty and a sense of status motivated this requirement which he imposed on his wife .... Alois dominated his wife even more completely than was customary in the 'authoritarian family structure' so beloved by sociologists. She owed everything to him, and, in her dependence, had nothing to counter his power. She had even been deprived of the period of give-and-take during the early years of marriage which provides maneuvering room for a wife in the most autocratic families. Alois had brought her into the household to fill a gap in the machine, and she never overcame this humble beginning. The peculiar background she shared with Alois also worked against her over the years. Even among her own close relatives, Alois was a more important figure than she.[10]

But not only did Klara suffer Alois' dominance and exploitation, she knew of his disloyalty. She must have known what awaited her when Alois made her pregnant at the time that his second wife, "Fanny," was dying of tuberculosis under the same roof. It is possible that Alois continued to have mistresses after his marriage to Klara, this being the more likely—and, in Alois' eyes, justified—as his official moves and duties kept him away from home for long periods. At one time he was transferred to Linz, and the family was left behind in Passau for one whole year, during which time he saw them only rarely. (On the other hand, Alois was then 57 and for this reason perhaps less likely to have carried on with women than in his heyday.) But for Klara, these and other absences of Alois must have meant, above all, relief, and must have given her the chance to turn her affections, concerns, and expectations more than ever onto Adolf, her only surviving son and delegate.

KLARA'S NEEDS FOR ADOLF

Given her personality and her marital situation, Klara could not help but channel major needs onto Adolf:

There was, first, her need to make up for the deprivation she herself had suffered as a child and was still suffering. Many mothers, we know from clinical practice, try to fulfill this need by "giving to their children" as they themselves needed to be given to. Some of these mothers become over gratifying juggernauts who stuff and spoil their children regardless of what the latter need, or do not need, in their own right. Klara seems to have been one of them.

Such a need to give, originating from her deprivation, might have resonated with her need to prove to herself and others that she was good, caring, and motherly—despite and because of her gnawing inner doubts. Thus, she attempted to benumb a hostile, albeit unconscious, ambivalence felt toward a child who, she sensed, enslaved her, sucked her dry, and crippled her with never-ending demands. But also, the need to constantly prove her goodness may have served to combat deep—and equally unconscious—guilt and shame (to be more fully explored in Chapter IV) that arose when she, a lodger and maid in her uncle's house, had with him an (almost) incestuous affair while his legitimate wife was still around, though dying. To lose her first three children in rapid succession may have signaled to her God's punishment and wrath, the more so as her stepchildren—born by Franziska—survived. No wonder that Klara not only overfed Adolf, but anxiously hovered over him, desperately needing him as living proof of her being a good, giving, non-destructive mother whom God still loved.

Further—responding to Adolf's stirring vitality—she very likely foisted upon him her hopes of finding through him some of the excitement, sense of importance, and power that she, the humble peasant woman, despaired of realizing by her own efforts, as her dreams for a fulfilling marriage turned increasingly to dust. In a sense, she recruited Adolf as fighter for her "Lebensraum," i.e., as a delegate who competed on her behalf for a share of the scarce—material as well as non-material—goods of the world.

Finally, sensing the boy's forceful self-assertiveness, she possibly recruited him to defeat, if not destroy, her exploiting and disloyal husband—even though, and probably because, she overtly remained to the end Alois' submissive maid.

In brief, I believe that Adolf, as Klara's loyal delegate, had to fulfill four major missions: First, the mission to "give by receiving," i.e., to absorb his mother's regressive gratification and, in so doing, to nurture *her*—a mission he could execute only by remaining deeply dependent on, and close to, her; second, the mission to be the living proof of her worthiness as mother; third, the mission to furnish Klara's life, through his exploits, with importance, excitement, and power by proxy; and, finally, the mission to serve as ally, avenger, and redeemer in her underhanded struggles with her oppressive and disloyal husband.

A LOOK AT ANOTHER DELEGATING MOTHER IN HISTORY

In Klara's relationship with Adolf, I must infer the delegating process from sparse and questionable data. For there exist, I noted earlier, no written documents that reveal how Klara's deeper fantasies, needs, and wishes bore on Adolf. It is different with another delegating mother who also fatefully influenced history.

I have in mind the mother of John Wilkes Booth, who assassinated Lincoln. P. Weissman (1964) has analyzed the available documents and perceptively traced the delegating process that operated between mother and son.

According to the memoirs of Booth's sister, Asia Booth Clarke—released for publication in 1938—Booth's mother impressed on her son a fantasy she had when he was six months old, which seems to have haunted her and him ever after. Thus Asia tells us that

> . . . his mother, when he was a babe of six months old, had 'a vision' in answer to a fervent prayer in which she imagined that the foreshadowing of his fate had been revealed to her, and as this incident was more painfully impressed upon her mind by a 'dream' when he had attained manhood, both vision and dream were familiarized to me by frequent repetition. . . . The oft-told reminiscence was put into this form and presented to the mother on her *birthday;* the lines claim no other *merit* than affording an explanation of her vision:

THE MOTHER'S VISION
Written 1854, June 2nd,
by A. B. (Asia Booth), Hartford Co., Md.

'Tween the passing night and the coming day
When all the house in slumber lay,

A patient mother sat low near the fire,
With that strength even nature cannot tire,
Nursing her fretful babe to sleep—
Only the angels these records keep
   Of mysterious love!

One little confiding hand lay spread
Like a white-oped lily, on that soft bed,
The mother's bosom, drawing strength and contentment warm—
The fleecy head rests on her circling arm.
In her eager worship, her fearful care,
Riseth to heaven a wild, mute prayer
   Of foreboding Love!

Tiny, innocent white baby-hand,
What force, what power is at your command,
For evil, or good? Be slow or be sure,
Firm to resist, to pursue, to endure—
My God, let me see what this hand shall do
In the silent years we are tending to;
   In my hungering Love,
I implore to know on this ghostly night
Whether 'twill labour for wrong, or right,
For—or against Thee?

     The flame up-leapt
Like a wave of blood, an avenging arm crept
Into shape; and COUNTRY shone out in the flame,
Which fading resolved to her boy's own name!
God had answered love—
   Impatient Love![1] [1]

   To quote Weissman,

This is the terrible vision of John's destiny, written as a poem for the mother's birthday by sister Asia when she was withteen and John sixteen. The vision implies an early death, an act of brave but bloody violence, in the name of the Country. However, its morality is in doubt—'for wrong or right,' 'For—or against Thee?" Asia further tells us, 'Mother and I often talked of her "vision in the fire" and of her "awful dream". . .' John Wilkes was not spared from hearing this 'talk' and became intensely preoccupied with its content.[1] [2]

As with Adolf Hitler, John Wilkes Booth's mission (to kill Lincoln) needs to be understood within a complex family scenario, which Weissmann unravels.

HITLER'S ADOLESCENCE RECONSIDERED

Adolf's missions as described above would, we notice at once, have been almost impossible to reconcile. The first two would have required that Adolf remain deeply bound to his mother—bound on an id as well as superego (i.e., archaic loyalty) level; bound as a spoilt (i.e., regressively gratified) child; and as a loyalty-bound youngster who reeled under breakaway guilt. The other two missions, in contrast, would have required Adolf to move out of her orbit so as to furnish her life with glamour and meaning, to realize her expectations of worldly success, and to become her avenger and redeemer. In trying to succeed as her delegate, he thus would have been subject to conflicts of missions and conflicts of loyalties, as earlier described; yet conflicts so deep and intense as to derail, if not thwart, the delegating process.

Is there evidence that Adolf Hitler suffered these conflicts and that the delegating process was derailed? I believe there is. To find it, we must once more return to Hitler's adolescence.

Adolescence, we know, is a time of reckoning—for parents and separating children. Yet, although two parties are involved, only one party—the separating child—has so far been the focus of extensive psychoanalytic studies; most psychoanalytic authors have conceptualized the vicissitudes of this period from the vantage point of the separating adolescent only.

When we view the adolescent as delegate of his parents, the conflict scenario widens. It now spans the intrapsychic as well as interpersonal realms, and encompasses parents and adolescents, delegators and delegates. Here we focus on the adolescent Adolf as delegate of his mother.

ADOLF BOUND BY REGRESSIVE GRATIFICATION

As an adolescent, Adolf exemplified many features I came to observe and expect in id-bound—regressively gratified—adolescents. He took for granted that his mother and sister Paula would dote on him, clean up after him, settle his expenses, and not seriously require him to work, to study hard, or to earn his keep.

This is in accord with the account of William Patrick Hitler of how his father—Alois, Jr.—viewed his younger half-brother:

As Adolf became older he was still excused from doing any unpleasant chores. He always claimed to be sick and his mother kept him in bed a good part of the time and even carried his meals to him there. He was pampered from early morning until late at night and the step-children had to listen to endless stories about how wonderful Adolf was and about what a great painter he would be some day.[12a]

Not surprisingly, Adolf failed in the *Realschule*, which demanded harder study than the *Völksschule*. (In addition, self-defeat probably played a role here, as we shall see shortly.) The picture of the spoiled son accords further with that of the dandy who paraded himself in Linz with cane, frock coat, top hat and kid gloves, who expected to be admired and noticed not for what he did but for what he was or appeared to be. It accords also with that of the ever greedy, restless, and stimulus-hungry boy who needed to experience, absorb, and devour everything—books, ideas, operas, plays—that came into his reach, yet was unable to stick to anything, to exert efforts or to endure frustration, who expected to have everything "served on a silver platter." At one point, we learn from Kubizek, he anticipated a sure win in a lottery, planned his life accordingly, and responded with rageful disbelief when his ticket lost. Also, being id-bound, he had no real friends—at least friends that made demands, as no peer or alternate adult could have matched his mother's total and unconditional devotion—with the sole exception of the ever submissive August Kubizek, his only friend in those friendless years, and, in fact, the only peer with whom he could use the informal *"Du"* (you) rather than the formal *"Sie"* (thou).[13] Further, Adolf's retreat into fantasies and grandiose schemes—indulged in while staying close to his mother—reflected such id-level boundless, as did his excessive irritability, his fits of rage, his tendency to blame everybody and anything. As I have described elsewhere (1973a, 1974c), id-bound children, their will to separate sapped, easily gain the power to make their own as well as their parents' lives unendurable. Here, as their awakened—libidinal and aggressive—drives have no objects other than their parents, they again confront dangerously reactivated preoedipal and oedipal conflicts. Inevitably, these parents (particularly the parent of the opposite sex) become targets of renewed symbiotic and/or incestuous pulls, replete with anxieties and conflicts. And inevitably, these anxieties and conflicts intensified for Adolf when he became closely locked in not only with his mother but also with his father after the latter retired from official duties.

HITLER SUBJECT TO BREAKAWAY GUILT

Unconscious breakaway guilt, I said earlier, afflicts those deeply loyalty-bound adolescents whose every attempt to separate—in thought or action—subjectively amounts to the heinous crime of murdering their binding parent (or parents). My work with schizophrenic patients, especially, has taught me how fiercely and relentlessly such unconscious guilt operates. In general, massively loyalty-bound adolescents try to cope with such guilt in any of three ways, all well known in psychoanalytic practice: by defeating themselves, by ferociously attacking or blaming others, or by craving atonement and repair work. As an adolescent, Hitler evinced mainly the first two mechanisms. He defeated himself (more or less unconsciously) when he failed not only in what others wanted him to do—to get along in school or embark on a conventional career—but also in what he himself (consciously) had set out to achieve—artistic success and renown. Rather than pursuing these goals wholeheartedly, he idled and procrastinated, an emotionally and intellectually retarded youngster. As such, he made sure he would stay with his mother, and thus avoid breakaway guilt. When, after her death, he finally moved to Vienna, he continued to fail as an artist. At the same time—if we believe the portrait drawn by Kubizek[14]—he blamed and attacked others, such as school authorities, the rotten Austrian state, stupid academicians, teachers, intellectuals, socialists, Jews, pacifists, with increasing ferocity, and thereby tried to appease his guilt. It was only after his mother's death that he could also use the third major mechanism—seeking heroic repair and atonement—to cope with his breakaway guilt, as we shall shortly see.

ADOLF DELEGATED TO SEEK IMPORTANCE AND POWER

Was Adolf, bound and reeling under breakaway guilt, also delegated as his mother's thrill-provider and seeker of power? I believe he was, even though my evidence is indirect. Essentially, I rely here on my experience with many subdued, self-effacing parents, particularly home-bound mothers, seen over months and years of family therapy, who covertly encouraged their children to do what they themselves never dared to do—e.g., be reckless, provocative, or defiant—and to achieve what they themselves were never able to achieve—e.g., become famous, powerful, important. Certainly, we shall never know for sure what Klara felt when she confronted Adolf's vitality, magnetism, and vivid imagination—features that he revealed early on and that were apparent throughout his childhood and adolescence—but, if clinical experience is a guide, she foisted on these features her own thwarted hopes and desires. If so, she recruited him, indeed, as her delegate—entrusting him with missions that required him to (conditionally) leave her orbit, while, on other levels, she bound him ever more tightly to her, as we saw.

ADOLF AS HIS MOTHER'S AVENGER

As his mother's ally, Adolf, very likely, came to view his father primarily as Klara's oppressor and exploiter, but also as possessor of autocratic power—something he resented, feared, and desired at one and the same time. To serve here as Klara's delegate, Hitler would have had to fight her battles and—more or less underhandedly—defeat his father. However, as an adolescent, Adolf seemed not yet able to do so. To be sure, he fought his father passively, as when he refused to study seriously at the *Realschule*[15] and resisted the career that Alois favored, but any wish to destroy his father seemed checked by Adolf's need to retain him as respected parent, male model, and limit-setting executive. The available evidence suggests that Adolf approached his father—as well as later father-substitutes, including some teachers, army officers, and finally President Hindenburg[16]—with precariously ambivalent attitudes. These included idealization, obsequiousness, and, as time went by, increasing resentment, contempt, daring defiance, and vindictive fury.

The wish to defeat or destroy one parent on behalf of the other cannot but rebound on the destroyer. Hamlet, hovering on the brink of schizophrenia and finally inviting his own destruction, provides a paradigm here. In such conflicts of loyalties there can be only losers, for if the child succeeds in destroying one parent—particularly the parent of the opposite sex—on behalf of the other, guilt will haunt him, and he will consume himself in hatred of self and of the other parent, whose ally and delegate he was. Yet such a tragic course, I believe, was staked out for Adolf, and we shall see later how it unfolded.

Hitler's adolescence drew to a close at about the time when his mother approached a torturous death. But before we turn to this event, let us pause and go back briefly to one source on Adolf's adolescence.

Illustration 1 – Hitler's Adolescent Poem (published with the permission of Bundesarchiv Koblenz)

A GLIMPSE INTO AN ADOLESCENT'S MIND

The earliest extant document from Hitler's hands is, strangely enough, a poem. It was found in a country inn, scrawled in its guestbook. Apparently Adolf wrote it ten days after his sixteenth birthday, i.e., at the age when, according to his latter-day reminiscences, "all young people write poetry."[17] It was also the age at which he—if we trust those reminiscences—came closest to the stereotype of a boisterous, "rebellious" adolescent. It was then that he spent his last year at the *Realschule* in Steyr mocking teachers, playing pranks (on one occasion even using his report card as toilet paper) and getting drunk at least once. But as I said earlier, such adolescent rebelliousness may also grow chiefly out of a delegating process—as when a son has to provide a parent with vicarious excitement or must act out the parent's disowned delinquent and rebellious impulses. And Hitler's poem from the Steyr period lends credence, I believe, to this assumption, since it accords generally with my view of Adolf as his mother's bound delegate. Therefore let us now examine it.

Even though it is not completely decipherable, it affords perhaps the most direct though fleeting glimpse into his state of mind and fantasies during his growing years. As an offshoot of his unconscious, it compares with passages quoted earlier from *Mein Kampf* which I—along with Kurth and Langer—suspect to reveal central childhood experiences. But it is, of course, more freshly revealing, for he wrote *Mein Kampf* as an adult—i.e., when he was far removed from the events of his formative period.

Here the German original—which appears for the first time in print[18]—is followed by my English translation, in which I have tried to convey the poet's clumsy style as well as his message.

Da sitzen die Menschen im luftigen Haus
Sich labend an Weinen und Bieren
Und essen und saufen in Saus und Braus
*[...] * hinaus dann auf allen den vieren*

Da kraxeln sie hohe Berge hinauf
*[...] * mit stolzem Gesichte*
Und kugeln hinunter in purzelndem Lauf
Und finden kein gleiches Gewichte.

Und komen sie traurig zu Hause an
Und sind dann vergessen die Stunden
dann komt [...] * sein Weib [...] * Mann
Und heilt ihm mit Prügeln die Wunden

von Adolf Hitler*[1][9]

[On the Damberg (near Steyr), 30 April 1905. Entry into a
guest book.][2][0]

People sit there in the airy house
Feasting on wines and beers
And eat and drink without a pause
[...] * till they can't raise their rears.

Up the higher mountains they strut
[...] * their faces so proud and daring
And then they roll down, a bouncing lot
And cannot regain their bearings.

And once they sadly at home arrive
And the hours have been forgotten
Then comes to the man [...] * his wife [...] *
And heals with thrashings his bottom.[2][1]

by Adolf Hitler

What, then, does the poem tell us about young Adolf?
Obviously, he takes off from what he sees around him: a country
inn filled with eating and drinking people. Tuned into this
conviviality, he dwells, in the first stanza, on the delight as well as
the pitfalls of excessive oral gratification. His language is gross, if
not vulgar, its forced humor reflecting unease and contempt. This
fits the picture of an overindulged, id-bound boy who craves, as
well as detests, being indulged.

In the second stanza, the focus shifts away from oral themes:

Adolf now derides all those who overconfidently aim at too lofty heights and then tumble down, a ridiculous bunch. Here, it appears, Adolf projects onto others his exorbitant ambitions, yet is also afraid of defeat and ridicule—ambitions and fears that I linked to his role as Klara's power- and fame-seeking delegate.

Finally, he gleefully expands on the plight of these fallen heroes and thereby again shifts his focus. They have no loving wives to comfort them; their wives "heal their wounds with beatings." What accounts for this turn of Adolf's imagination? To understand it I believe we must remind ourselves, first of all, of what he experienced in Steyr. Here he witnessed how his landlady pitilessly browbeat her hapless husband, as Hitler gleefully recalled in his Secret Conversations of January 9, 1942.[22] But the whole tone and development of the poem, and especially the use of the word *Prügeln*" (thrashings, beatings), cause me to think that his landlandy and her spouse were mere stand-ins for more important dramatis personae—his parents. To grasp the central concern of the last stanza, we must, I believe, go back to the fact that Adolf, according to various testimony, was beaten frequently by his father. We must further keep in mind that the feasting people around him were, most likely, men who, removed from their women's reproach and envy, enjoyed a boastful "homoerotic" intimacy, perhaps replete with hostile sexual as well as sexist jokes. This would have been like many scenes that even today unfold in countless country inns throughout the German-speaking—in fact, the Western—world. If so, the main question would be: why did Adolf take the wives', and not the men's, side?

I believe that here again the answer lies in his relationship with Klara. Very likely, when his father beat him, it was she who "healed his wounds." Now, in his fantasies, he acts as her loyal ally and delegate, and makes her triumph over a husband who comes across as weak, pretentious, and ridiculous. In this way, he affirms Klara as the parent with the "stronger reality" (Stierlin, 1959). At the same time, he foreshadows his mission as her fiercely avenging delegate, which will occupy us in later pages.

SEPARATION FROM HIS DYING MOTHER

Here we must recall the chronology of events: in May-June 1906, Adolf, then 17 years old, made his first visit to Vienna.

In January 1907, Dr. Bloch diagnosed his mother's breast cancer.

In early October 1907, Hitler took the entrance examination for the Vienna Academy of Fine Arts, but failed.

On December 21, 1907, his mother died.

While there is still some question about the exact date of Hitler's return from Vienna[23]—after he was examined at the Academy of Fine Arts—there can be no doubt that, during that one year, he was mostly in close contact with his mother, that her terminal illness and eventual death pervaded all he did and thought, and caused him the deepest concerns and conflicts. Essentially, these arose out of his condition as a "bound delegate" and involved the following: concerns over losing that person who, in unstinting devotion, had indulged him and who, in binding and delegating him, had caused him to feel unique, important, and "chosen"; hate for this very same person who, in her binding and delegating of him, had also lived through him, i.e., had exploited and suffocated him. Hence his ambivalent wish to lose and not lose her, to fear and wish her death, to maintain symbiotic closeness and yet find liberation. No doubt, his mother's terminal illness, drawn out over almost a year, mirrored and highlighted what he most deeply feared and wished, thus magnifying his breakaway guilt, the more so as his moves to Vienna might well have speeded—if not contributed to—Klara's succumbing to cancer. In my personal and clinical experience, I have observed repeatedly how seemingly "straight" organic diseases such as cancer originated, improved, or worsened in the context of vital family dynamics.[24]

Be this as it may, Adolf must have perceived his mother in the autumn of 1907 in a manner similar to Kubizek, who recalled:

Frau Klara seemed more depressed than usual. Her face was deeply lined, her eyes were lifeless and her tone of voice was weary and resigned. She gave me the impression, now that Adolf was no longer living with her, of having completely let herself go, and she looked older and more of an invalid than before. To make it easier for her son to go, she had undoubtedly concealed her condition from him . . . but now that she was on her own she seemed to me an old and ailing woman.[25]

In other words, Adolf, too, must have perceived his mother in ways that could not but maximize his conflicts and breakaway guilt. It seems that he tried to reduce his guilt by pressuring Dr. Bloch into a useless treatment and by tenderly nursing his sick mother. But neither, it appears, was enough to resolve the ambivalence, conflicts of missions, and conflicts of loyalties that nourished his guilt. It was only approximately twelve years later, within the scenario that Binion described—now emerging as the bound and binding delegate of his new "mother" Germany—that Adolf got a new chance to resolve his separation conflicts—this time in ways that affected millions of people and the course of history. To gain a better understanding of what happened then, I shall next look at Hitler as an artist who, in his very attempt to liberate himself and to solve his most central conflicts, destroyed himself and countless others.

CHAPTER III

HITLER AS CREATIVE AND DESTRUCTIVE ARTIST

Artists evoke mostly positive associations in us. These relate to how they enrich the world, give rise to new sensibilities, and consume themselves while creating; in brief, we like to view them as heroes. Given this common tendency, what follows might seem strange. For I shall not extoll such positive aspects, but explore some destructive features that artists not seldom reveal. Such a focus does not detract from the gifts for which mankind owes much to them. Rather, it balances our appreciation of these with an awareness of creativity's frequently exorbitant toll—extracted not only from many artists themselves, but also from others who enter their orbits.

My awareness of this toll heightened the more I came to know the families and important relations of such artists—patients as well as literary figures—and found them to be human disaster areas. Specifically, I noted how these artists' conflicts, and especially those over their separation, caused them massively to exploit others. And the more I studied Hitler, the more I found him to exemplify at least some of those destructive and exploitative dynamics which, in other artists—who are so much more appealing and human than Hitler—can easily be condoned. Hence arose the plan for this chapter.

What case, then, can be made for Hitler as artist? We know from

Speer (1970) and others that Hitler, up to his final months, even though he was no longer painting or drawing, viewed himself as an artist. But may *we* view him as such and, most important, may we call him creative? I believe we can, even though, at first sight, several arguments contradict such a notion. Essentially, these arguments run as follows: First, we have come to associate creativity with moral values and redeeming human features such as compassion, kindness, humor, forgiveness. But of these, it is said, Hitler had none. Second, when we speak of artistic creativity, we require evidence of truly original achievements. Yet these, we hear, Hitler failed to produce. For, even though he left hundreds of paintings and drawings behind, none of them had distinctive or lasting value. And, third, granted even that he was in some ways creative, so the argument runs, such creativity was eclipsed by his destructiveness.

Yet these arguments are valid only up to a point, as closer inspection shows. Faced with the first argument—concerning moral values and redeeming features—we must ask whether Hitler simply lacked these, or whether he hid or distorted them; whether he, as a mere cynical manipulator, exemplified and stirred only base instincts, or whether he, in (to him) good faith, also embodied and appealed to the highest, self-transcending motives. I, for one, would argue the latter. For while I do not doubt an historian's statement that "Hitler was convinced that every man had his price, and [that] he had a flair for sensing what that price might be, whether it was peace, power, status, money, or simply personal security,"[1] I am also prepared to argue (and shall do so in subsequent chapters) that his appeal had moral bases, too, skewed and distorted as these might have been. Here I draw support from A. Koestler (1968) who asserts "the damages wrought by individual violence . . . are insignificant compared to the holocausts resulting from self-transcending devotion to collectively shared belief systems."[2] Essentially, I believe that Hitler, in order to kindle such belief systems, had to be a self-transcending believer himself.

Faced with the second argument—concerning Hitler's originality—we must ask for criteria by which to judge it. Specifically, we must define the field (or fields) of art in which he labored. To be sure, if we judge him within those established fields he himself had originally chosen—painting and architecture—claims for originality are hard to maintain. For, even though respectable experts acknowledged his talents[3]—as when they praised some of his World War I drawings and water colors—on the whole he failed, and still fails, to inspire or excite by what he produced as painter or architect.

But rather than considering his water colors and drawings we must, I believe, assess Hitler's artistic creativity within a field that he himself staked out and which still lacks a good name. I have in mind one in which at least three major endeavors, all deserving the name of "arts," are conjoined: the art of power politics, played on the smallest and largest scales; the art of "political stagecrafting"; and the art of myth-making or, better, myth-selling. In welding together these fields, Hitler resembled Wagner, his much admired model, who also uniquely integrated musical compositions, playwriting, and stagecrafting into a *Gesamtkunstwerk*,[4] thus creating a new art form.

To excel in Machiavellian politics, Hitler had to be a passionate seeker and a coldly calculating technician of power. He was both. To excel as political stagecrafter, he had to be a successful orator and an actor, which he was. (In the words of the historian A. Bullock [1962] he "was the greatest demagogue in history."[5]) Also, he had to possess a sure instinct for effective stage designs, groupings, rituals, symbols, and slogans. Here, too, he was unmatched. Whether it was his choice of the Swastika for Germany's banner, his careful build-up of suspense during a beer hall speech, or his masterminding the gigantic Nuremberg rallies, in all he demonstrated his genius for manipulating passions and for keeping his audiences in captive trances. And, finally, to excel as maker and salesman of myths, he had to articulate a vision, or *Weltanschauung*, that was simple, coherent, convincing, and geared to his followers' deepest needs. Here again he succeeded superbly, as E. Jäckel (1972) has shown.

Faced, finally, with the third argument—that Hitler's destructiveness overshadowed his creativity—we must ask the question that is central to this chapter: How did Hitler, in creatively solving his most basic conflicts, bring about his own and others' destruction?

THE INTERWEAVING OF LIBERATING AND CREATIVE FORCES IN THE CHILD

To pursue this question, I shall now take off from a phenomenon which the late D. W. Winnicott described. I have in mind what he called *transitional objects* (1953), which figure centrally in a child's first separation from his mother. Typically, they are objects such as blankets, dolls, or teddy bears that, to the child, come to embody his mother's attributes, particularly her warmth and protective presence. These objects allow the child to hang onto his mother in a concrete way, but also to control and manipulate her. We can say that he now has the best of two worlds. He carries his mother with him, as it were, yet can also get rid of her when he wishes; he has autonomy, yet can also bask in dependence. In this way, the child makes a decisive liberative move.

At the same time—and this is important—the child also achieves a creative feat, for he reconciles what seems irreconcilable, namely autonomy and dependence. The reconciliation of the seemingly irreconcilable in a new and usually more intricate pattern (be this behavioral, relational, or esthetic) is, I believe, the essence of the creative process. Thus, by recruiting transitional objects, the child embarks on a liberative, as well as creative, venture.

THE CRITICAL THRESHOLD

As he matures, the child reaches a threshold at which his creativity and liberation may surge (yet also may subsequently falter). This is when he begins to move into the world of words and symbols, when he begins to appropriate his culture through fairy tales, nursery rhymes, myths, and similar elements. To understand what this involves, we must turn to some other observations of Winnicott's—those pertaining to what he variously called the area of cultural activity, of play, or of artistic illusion (1967). (H. Linche [1973] a Swiss psychoanalyst, has further expounded this subject.) Winnicott located this area between the areas of "subjective experience," as obtaining in dreams and fantasies, and of "objective experience," as shaped by societal institutions and language (which Hegel, in 1810, called the realm of the "objective spirit"). Therefore, Winnicott spoke here also of the "intermediate area." Within this intermediate area, transitional objects increasingly lose their concreteness, i.e., teddy bears become pictures of teddy bears and pictures of teddy bears become words or symbols representing teddy bears. These words and symbols can still powerfully evoke the mother's warmth and presence as well as innumerable other things, yet allow even more leeway for manipulation and reconciliation than do concrete teddy bears and blankets.

In introducing this intermediate area, Winnicott brought into view some of the dilemmas we must face when we want to liberate ourselves and also want to be—or remain—creative.

First, he made understandable why human beings, as children, almost cannot *not* be creative, for all children are plunged head-on into this intermediate area, as it were. While their world still glows with pristine brilliance, and emotional currents still break forth easily, they must, willy-nilly, create meaning by linking new images, new things, and new words (even though, or because, they often cannot yet distinguish between the three). Hence the frequent originality of their utterances, hence the freshness of their paintings and drawings, hence the inventiveness of their play, hence their charm.

But as they grow older—and this, too, appears to follow from Winnicott's observations—children seem to find it increasingly difficult to operate creatively in the intermediate area: they are pulled either into the area of purely subjective experience—the area bounded by dreams or fantasies—or into that of objective experience—that bounded by traditional patterns of thought and action. In either case, they lose their creative edge.

To be sure, not a few people dispute the above and consider dreaming and fantasizing to be creative activities. For example, they hold that in dreaming we all turn into creative visionaries and playwrights, as we conjure images resplendent with meaning, plot bold dramas, connect the seemingly unconnectable, speak the unspeakable, reveal whilst we conceal, and display an ingenuity that later makes us and our analyst marvel.

Yet the creativity of dreamers, we know, tends to wither quickly under waking life's glare. Only rarely does the creative momentum of dreams carry over into immediate wakeful productivity as it did for Kekulé when he found the formula of the benzene ring in 1865. (This applies also to states of altered consciousness—such as those caused by LSD, marijuana, or peyote—which resemble dream states and which, like dreams, seem to unleash creative forces. Here, also, visions emerge out of the soul's archaic layers, colors intensify, new links and meanings appear, and horizons expand. Yet here again the creative surge—if we can call it that—tends to falter soon and ordinarily does not produce lasting achievement. On the contrary, many drug users, huddling together more and more passively, seem increasingly to lose their zest for life.) Thus, while dreams may have the emotional charge and imaginative power of true art, they seem too far removed from the realm of durable, objective experience—the realm of enduringly shared words, symbols, and experiential structures—to deserve the name of creative achievements.

But those human productions that adhere too greatly to such objective experience, that fit in too closely with established modes of thought and perception, also do not impress us as creative just because they remain stuck in well-worn tracks. Creativity, it follows, remains precariously lodged in Winnicott's intermediate area, combining in a unique mixture that which is private *and* public, real *and* illusionary, subjective *and* objective, and this mixture, evidently, is hard to achieve.

THE ARTIST'S TASK OF RECONCILIATION

Still, certain individuals—whom we call creative artists—do achieve it and Hitler, I submit, must be counted among them. These artists refuse to be dislodged from the intermediate realm, even while they grow older. They neither merely dream nor merely follow established tracks. Rather, they remain foragers into, or conquistadors of, the intermediate realm and get away with it. How do they do it?

They must, first of all, remain childlike in important respects. Like children, they seem to retain the capacity to see our modern-day emperors without clothes: they are not fooled by clichés, or the glitter of wealth, or power, or conventionally shared sentimentalities. In important respects they avoid being blunted by the process of so-called education.

But being or remaining childlike is not enough. To become and stay creative, artists must possess an elusive commodity called "talent." Even more important, they must be able to reconcile several structural contradictions that seem built into the creative process. Thus, they must be able to pursue and mold their personal vision in the face of inevitable criticism, misunderstanding, or nonrecognition—the more so the more novel or daring their vision. They must have a capacity for defiant loneliness, as it were, a basic, stubborn, self-confidence, which sustains them *coûte que coûte*. And yet they must reach out to others and communicate their vision in ways that eventually so grip or seduce these others that they come to share and appropriate it.

To do all these things, the artist must, as a rule, become totally absorbed in his private project, yet also must keep a foot in the public world; he must tune himself to his unconscious processes to an unusual extent, yet must also check them against reality (or, better, against what others hold to be reality). In brief, he must use his creativity for the purpose of being with, as well as without, others, thus heeding Goethe, who said: "Man can find no better retreat from the world than art, and man can find no stronger link with the world than art."

LIBERATION FROM THE BAD MOTHER AND FAMILY

To explore further this difficult venture of reconciliation, and to make it applicable to Hitler, let me once more return to the toddler and his transitional objects. This toddler, we saw, liberated himself from his mother by packaging her desirable attributes into his blanket or teddy bear, while he got rid of undesirable ones. He creatively transformed his mother, as it were, as he split her up into several components, some good and retainable, others bad and disposable—as he made her movable and brought her under the spell of his imagination.

But such creative transformation of mother, we must now remind ourselves, has its limits; limits to be found in the child *and* in his mother. The child is limited insofar as his potential for creative liberation, while impressive, also remains precariously circumscribed, for whatever he does, he still needs his real mother (and needs her for a long time to come). He needs her protective shelter, her material and emotional nurturance, her cognitive guidance; and, perhaps most important, he needs her to find *him* important; he needs her to love him, not because he deserves it, but because he is there, a little child.

This, then, brings into view those limits on his liberative efforts that are set by his mother—as when she fails to provide shelter, or fails to give proper nurturance or guidance, or fails to bestow on him a deep sense of importance. When this happens, the child's plight worsens. Not only must he liberate himself from his (to use another of Winnicott's terms) "not-good-enough-mother"; he must also make up, as much as he can, for her failings. He must become his own emotional repair man. He must find a creative solution not only to the dependence-independence dilemma described earlier, but also to his emotional deprivation, or harmful overstimulation, or mystification by his mother, or whatever the case might be.

And, insofar as the mother operates in an interpersonal field that includes her husband and the rest of the family, the repair work must encompass them, too.

This, then, brings us back to Adolf Hitler and his conflicts, as these relate to his mother and other family members. How, we ask now, did Hitler, as creative artist, tackle the reconciliation that such conflicts seem to demand? To find our way here, let us look more closely at what this reconciliation implied for him.

THE RESURRECTION AND TRANSFORMATION OF MOTHER

The first and most momentous step in the reconciliation was for Hitler to resurrect his mother. This he did when, as Binion showed, he "transferred to Germany all his affectivity unconsciously attached to his mother"[6] and made his motherland his "only bride."[7] But in this process he also transformed his mother—in fantasy, as well as reality. He now manipulated Germany as a transitional object that afforded more leeway for solving conflicts than his actual mother ever could.

CONQUISTADOR IN THE INTERMEDIATE AREA

Yet to exploit such leeway, it was not enough to merely adopt his new mother. He also had to secure a context—a shared and plausible vision of reality—that kept her alive. This meant he had to link the notion and myth of the German nation as mother to other supporting notions and myths. To this end, he had to delve further into the intermediate area. And this he did, as M. Eliade (1972), for one, has shown, by appropriating myths that people have shared throughout history. These included the myth that good and evil, dark and fair, eternally fight each other; that the chosen—i.e., the strong, loyal, and noble ones—enter the kingdom of Heaven, while the damned—i.e., the weak, disloyal, and slavish ones—must perish; and that there exists, somewhere, somehow, a Jerusalem, a sacred mother-city that requires holy war and sacrifice.

SALESMAN OF MYTHS

But to retrieve and update myths was not enough. In addition, Hitler had to achieve two things: discredit existing visions of reality, and promote the one *he* had gleaned from the intermediate area. The first required that he impede ordinary ways of categorizing, defining, and testing reality, and that, by stirring constant motion, he blur his followers' critical judgment. The second demanded that he force-feed them *his* vision, his *Weltanschauung*, a *Weltanschauung* that, to him, was the granite-hard fundament—*Das granitene Fundament*[8]—that guided all his actions. Its basic elements, we saw, were the notions of an eternal Darwinian struggle for survival and *Lebensraum* and of the necessity to destroy those who bypassed, perverted, or parasitically exploited his struggle: the Jews.

Equipped with this vision, Hitler could tackle anew those conflicts that his family had bequeathed him. Specifically, he could become newly bound-up with his mother and, out of such renewed boundness, could once again pursue those missions that were her legacy to him.

By becoming newly bound-up (or symbiotically fused) with Germany, he obtained strength, oral regressive gratification, orgiastic sexualized bliss, and a sense of being chosen, at one and the same time. Jubilantly he could assert, "I am Germany and Germany is I," and tell his cheering audiences "that is the miracle of our times that you have found me. And that I have found you, is Germany's joy and fortune."[9]

And in such blissful union he fulfilled, almost effortlessly it seemed, one of the missions Klara had entrusted to him: to lead his mother out of darkness and supply her with excitement, importance, and power, as he excited her and highlighted his and her power, in one new venture after another, be this through gigantic rallies, through sheer force and/or terror, or through projects of organization and conquest so large as to dwarf any comparisons.

In thus boosting Germany's importance and power, he laid the groundwork for executing another major mission—healing her wounds and making up for her early losses, i.e., reversing Germany's military defeat and recouping her lost territories which now were unconsciously equated with children: those children whom Klara had lost shortly before Adolf was born, and who were the reason for that maternal trauma which he, in the words of Binion, "sucked in . . . with his mother's milk."[10]

But further, by using large parts of the world as a gigantic participatory theatre, he embarked on one more mission to which he, as Klara's delegate and ally, was heir: to avenge her against her profiteering Jewish poisoner and, on a deeper level, against her oppressive husband, Adolf's father. It was a revenge grotesquely exaggerated and displaced, yet deadly effective.

A CAPACITY FOR DEFIANT LONELINESS

Like any artist, Hitler had to resolve those structural contradictions that we found built into the creative process: he had to reconcile a capacity for defiant loneliness and one for gripping and seducing others; he had to be totally absorbed in his artistic project and yet reach out to his audience. What do we find?

Clearly, Hitler was able to pursue and mold his personal vision in the face of criticism, misunderstanding, and nonrecognition as few, if any, others could have done. And he himself seems to have realized that such "heroic loneliness" was central to his eventual success, as he wrote in *Mein Kampf*:

> For the greater a man's works for the future, the less the present can comprehend them; the harder his fight, and the rarer success. If, however, once in centuries success does come to a man, perhaps in his latter days a faint beam of his coming glory may shine upon him. To be sure, these great men are only the marathon runners of history; the laurel wreath of the present touches only the brow of the dying hero.[11]

And, true to these words, he showed to the end an unyielding self-confidence, even when he was physically a broken man, prematurely senile, with stooped gait, one arm trembling, saliva running down his lips, and harrowed by military reverses. Even then his utterances, if not his demeanor, conveyed: "I never err. Each of my words is historical" (*Ich irre mich nie. Jedes meiner Worte ist historisch*).[12] It was, above all, this iron determination and display of unshakable confidence that turned ruthless and power-hungry strongmen into his spellbound followers, a quality over which Speer, for one, continued to marvel.[13]

A CAPACITY TO GRIP AND SEDUCE OTHERS

But a capacity for defiant loneliness, we saw, is not enough. To be successful, an artist must also be able to so grip or seduce others that they succumb to, and finally appropriate, his vision. And it is here that Hitler's perhaps most complex and formidable talents came into play. I have in mind his ability to open himself to his own, as well as his audiences', unconscious needs and conflicts and yet to balance such openness with disciplined detachment. This is one reason why, even today, observers disagree as to whether his rages and oratorical outbursts were genuine or play-acted, and whether even his hatred of Jews and Marxists was deeply felt or merely feigned. Yet it is exactly such a reconciliation of opposites that a creative artist has to achieve. He must be tuned to unconscious processes, yet not be carried away by them; he must feed on charged emotional material and yet reflect, mold, and transform this in the light of his overall vision. Seen from this vantage point, Hitler's often cited "icy biaslessness," his *"eiskalte Vorurteilslosigkeit,"* appears as a vital element in his artistic success. This *"eiskalte Vorurteilslosigkeit"* allowed him to evade the constraints of common sentimentalities, ordinary compassions, loyalties, and considerations of kindness and decency, as when he admiringly studied English World War I propaganda,[14] prided himself for learning even from Marxists and Jews, or disparaged the very formulations that Himmler and Rosenberg, his would-be ideologues, advanced to adorn the German people. (Thus, he mocked Himmler's contention that the early Germans had created civilizations comparable to those of Romans and Greeks;[15] rather, they had been barbarians, living in mud huts.) This ability sharply to detach himself from the very emotional forces he embodied goes a long way, I believe, to explain his ruthless, and finally destructive, efficiency. But so does his total absorption in his projects, the other ingredient in his creative efforts we need to consider.

TOTAL ABSORPTION IN HIS PROJECTS

An artist's creative effort must often be so total and exclusive that it thrives only at the expense of almost everything else. Nietzsche once said that any great talent makes a vampire of its owner: it feeds on everything—friends, family, the artist's physical and mental health. Therefore the world in which creative persons move is often strewn with the wreckage of ruined lives and hopes. From this point of view, it can be rightly said, as P. Weissman (1964), among others has done, that creativity is neither constructive nor adaptive in a conventional sense. The creative drive does not align itself with an ego that obeys a so-called reality principle, but rather seems captive to an unusually harsh and idiosyncratic superego that disregards all that may seem central to survival as well as elementary in human decency. To quote L.-F. Céline:

> Did I love Rosalie? The question is meaningless. When a man is desperately at odds with himself, others do not exist. He is a battlefield of principalities and powers. His relationships with others are a caricature of this conflict. He is alone. And the more people he knows, and the more famous he is, the greater the solitude. In all relations to others, I have been concerned only with myself.[16]

Here we find, then, I believe, one further reason for Hitler's lack of compassion and empathy, and for his cool destructiveness. Obsessed by his vision, and busily directing his gigantic participatory theatre, he viewed people as no more than actors, to be jugged, aroused, commandeered, and sent to their deaths as the director required. Therefore, he could be matter of fact, if not casual, about the deaths of millions of Jews and of countless Germans as well. When once, at the war's critical turning point, he learned of staggering losses among newly commissioned officers, he replied curtly: "Isn't that what the young people are there for!" (*"Aber dafür sind die jungen Leute doch da!"*)[17]

HITLER'S NARCISSISM

Psychoanalytic authors have evoked Hitler's narcissism to account for his lack of empathy and compassion. Fromm, in particular, we saw, made his narcissism into an encompassing explanatory formula. From the above vantage point, however, Hitler's narcissism appears a more complex, as well as more secondary, phenomenon than Fromm and others make it out to be. Rather than being a basic character trait, traceable to an early "malignant incestuousness" or other vicissitudes, I view it chiefly as a reflection of his total absorption in his missions. Most of the time these missions took total hold of him. When this happened, he could unblinkingly send thousands of soldiers and prisoners to their deaths. But even as party leader and later on as dictator, he could not always remain impervious to actual human suffering and at times was unable to maintain that precarious balance of dissociative and distortive processes that allowed him to treat the world as if it were mere theatre. I see here the main reason why Hitler avoided the sight of real corpses or executions, as Fromm mentions, for these would have jolted that balance. At least a few times it was, indeed, shattered so badly that reemerging conflicts and guilt brought him close to suicide. This happened, for example, when as a prisoner at Landsberg after the failure of the November *Putsch* of 1923, he temporarily fell out of his symbiosis with "mother Germany"; and later when "Geli" Raubal, his niece and mistress, killed herself and thereby ended an intensely possessive, sexualized, ambivalent, and quasi-incestuous relationship that evoked, repeated, and concealed what once—on the feeling level—had gone on between him and his mother.

We typically find a narcissism such as Hitler's in those bound delegates who must fulfill "missions impossible" and, at the same time, treat as an easily exploitable and discardable resource the human material of this world. Such narcissism, however, differs from the kind to be found under the expelling mode, as earlier described, where we deal with insidiously neglected and rejected individuals, those whom I called "wayward." As these wayward individuals appear unencumbered by common conventions, regulatory principles, bonds of loyalty, and hence by ordinary guilt, they too can exploit and discard people without qualms and, invading the intermediate area, can even succeed as artists. (I have observed this in treating a few of them and have reported on it elsewhere, 1974c.) But as they have no abiding missions to fulfill, they lack, most likely, a Hitler's dynamic appeal and passion.

SELF-DESTRUCTION IN THE CREATIVE PROCESS

An artist's destructive impact on others frequently matches, as well as reflects, that which he wreaks on himself. Various observers have commented on Hitler's drive for self-destruction and focused here on three aspects: his reckless risk-taking; his longing for, and preoccupation with, death; and his (covert) invitation to be punished and controlled. Fest, for one, emphasizes the first aspect, citing example after example of how Hitler, especially in the last years of the war, over played his cards and took risks that backfired. In the Eastern campaign, in particular, Hitler made one self-defeating, if not suicidal, decision after the other. In summing up here, Fest speaks of Hitler's "strategy of grandiose perdition" (*Strategie des grandiosen Untergangs*),[18] and of his "all-out will for catastrophe" (his *übergreifender Katastrophenwille*").[19]

Binion further illuminated Hitler's suicide strategy by linking it to his attempts to reverse Germany's World War I defeat. "Germany," he writes, "overestimated its own strength to a point of absurdity in the earlier play for world power—which was not a land grab primarily, or a *Drang nach Osten*, until huge vistas of Eastern conquest opened up in 1917 to 1918. Hitler ostensibly drew the consequence of the 1918 defeat when he urged a replay from a reduced power base and with the enlarged aim of world dominion," which was a sure recipe for military and national suicide.[20]

Further, Hitler's suicidal drive surfaced in a cult of death he celebrated in countless "liturgical rites," as when he orchestrated massive funeral processions or memorial services for war heroes and martyrs of the Nazi movement, complete with dipped banners, gigantic choruses, sombre marching music, and muted drums. Typically, Hitler preferred evening or night hours to stage his rallies and processinns, since a quality of moody darkness added to the effect. There was also his plan, divulged to Speer and others, to ring the far Eastern frontiers of the *Reich* with so-called *Todesburgen*—death castles—which were meant eternally to glorify heroic death, eternal struggle, and bloodshed. Not surprisingly, observers saw in all this an almost orgastic embrace of death, a *Todesrausch*, reminiscent of Richard Wagner, here again Hitler's model and mentor. And did not Hitler bring about his own *"Götterdämmerung"* and *"Niebelungentod"* when, in a finale as macabre as it was grandiose, holding center stage to the end, he blew his brains out, taking much of the theatre and its actors with him?

Finally, we recognize Hitler's drive for self-destruction in his constant, albeit covert, invitation to be punished and contained. The psychoanalytic literature amply describes this mechanism. A youngster, for example, laboring under vague but frighteningly intense guilt feelings, compulsively commits a crime—e.g., steals or wrecks a car—which precipitates the parents' punishment and thereby brings him relief for his guilt. It was Hitler's and Germany's problem here that for a long time no really limit-setting and punishing authority was forthcoming, and that it required the concerted efforts of much of the free world finally to slay him like a mad dog.

FURTHER OBSERVATIONS ON DESTRUCTIVENESS AND CREATIVITY

In Patrick White's *The Vivisector* (1970), a mother says of a young painter, "you were born with a knife in your hand, or rather in your eyes."[2][1] Many other authors have linked creativity to aggression and destruction. Adrian Stokes for one, emphasized that the sculptor begins his work by breaking and chipping the stone, or the painter by defiling the white canvas. Hitler, too, seems to have held that creation involves destruction.

In the foregoing I have argued that his own destructiveness as artist (aimed at others as well as himself) derived in large part from how he dealt with conflicts and missions that his parents, and particularly his mother, bequeathed him. Let me, then, mention two more self-destructive artists who, to me, revealed similar dynamics—artists who at first sight defy comparison with Hitler. I have in mind Friedrich Hölderlin and Franz Kafka, two of the greatest writers in the German language.

To be sure, the differences between them and Hitler could hardly seem larger. Hölderlin and Kafka were, after all, seminal artists who, unlike Hitler, produced original works of lasting value. And unlike Hitler, they were (largely) introverts, not outgoing political figures and movers of masses. But beside such obvious differences, I found similarities. For Kafka and Hölderlin too, I showed elsewhere (1972, 1974), attempted to resurrect and creatively transform the early mother-child symbiosis (or bind) and thereby they too forwarded their self-destruction—Hölderlin became mad in his mid-thirties,[22] and Kafka, not much older, died in the deep regressive self-abdication of tuberculosis.[23]

But here the similarities end. In dealing with Hitler, we face, above all, the issue of why his brand of "self-destructive creativity" engulfed countless others. To this the following two chapters seek answers.

CHAPTER IV

SHAME, GUILT, VENGEFULNESS, AND LOYALTY
IN HITLER'S MOTIVATIONS

CONTRASTING ARENAS FOR PSYCHOTIC CONFLICTS

Hölderlin's and Kafka's self-destruction implied a break with, as
well as a retreat from, so-called reality—features we commonly
associate with psychosis. With Hölderlin, the break and retreat
were massive enough to warrant the label of schizophrenia
(Stierlin, 1972b, 1973f); with Kafka, they were strong trends—as
his psychoanalytic biographer, John S. White (1967), has
documented. In either case, the psychotic drama of primitive
conflict, fragmentation, and dedifferentiation was played mainly
within one person: the artist himself.

Hitler, in contrast, synchronized his destruction with that of
others and, rather than breaking with—and away from—reality, he
made *his* reality theirs. Thereby he externalized, and also
transformed and widened, the arena of psychotic conflict. For, as
his "stronger reality" (Stierlin, 1959) abounded with irrationality
and contradiction, those who accepted it—or were forced to adjust
to it—became involved in nightmarish turmoil, while Hitler himself
could continue to function: he remained, as we saw, coherent and
in control to the end, even though stresses mounted and his body
threatened to break. In brief, he managed to evade personal
psychosis by fanning and sustaining collective psychosis.[1]

This feat he achieved through his formidable talents and strengths, mentioned earlier. But all these still seem insufficient to account for such an achievement. To achieve what he did, he not only had to stir powerful passions and exploit massive frustrations; he had to embody, and be able to tap, people's deepest convictions about what was right and just. To understand Hitler's "success" here, we must, I believe, above all else, consider the roles of shame, guilt, vengefulness, and loyalty in his motivational dynamics. To do so, let us begin by broadly examining the place of shame and guilt in human relations.

SHAME AND GUILT

Shame and guilt are central in human experience, just as they are in psychiatric theory and practice. They preoccupied philosophers such as Kierkegaard, Nietzsche, Sartre, Heidegger, Jaspers, as well as psychoanalysts such as Freud and Erikson, to name only a few. Both concepts denote painful and complex emotions. They relate to, and interweave with, each other, but also have different phenomenologies and dynamics. To understand shame and guilt in Hitler's life and relations, we must, first, briefly elaborate these differences.

THE DIFFERING PHENOMENOLOGIES AND DYNAMICS OF SHAME AND GUILT

Various psychoanalytic authors[2] have examined differences and similarities in the two phenomena. Shame and guilt, they concluded, while often appearing similar, differ with respect to common usage and ethnological roots.

Shame, essentially, implies painful embarrassment, humiliated fury, a sense of devastation and mortification often so deep that one wishes to sink into the ground. This feeling of shrinkage and diminution contrasts with the uplift that pride and triumph—the opposites of shame—provide.

Shame grows mainly out of competitive defeat, rebuff, and weakness, out of a sensed loss of self-control with accompanying loss of self-esteem. Also, shame seems specific to a sense of physical and sexual deficiency. A girl might feel ashamed because of her small breasts, her (assumed or real) sexual coldness or too ready arousal (which, to her, might indicate weakness); a boy because of his impotency, the small size of his penis, or exposure to sexual ineptitude. The German word *"Schamteile"* for genitals reflects the close affinity between sexual function or anatomy, and shame.

Guilt, in contrast, denotes the anguish and pain over hurting or wronging others or sacrosanct institutions such as the family, church, fatherland, etc. It seems specific to situations where we (in deeds or fantasy) attack, cheat, manipulate, humiliate, defy, envy,[3] those whom we believe or wish to love or obey. In brief, "guilt anxiety"—to use a formula of Piers and Singer (1953)—"accompanies transgression, shame, failure."[4]

Freud's constructs of the ego-ideal and superego (1914, 1923, 1933) illuminated the differing phenomenologies and dynamics of shame and guilt. Guilt and shame, Freud found, reflect, as well as generate, the tensions that arise between ego and ego-ideal (or superego). Freud clarified the nature of these tensions when he distinguished between the three superego functions of *ego-ideal, conscience,* and *self-observation* (1933).[5] Of these, the ego-ideal relates primarily to the experience of shame; conscience to that of guilt; while self-observation plays a central, though differing, role in shame *and* guilt. (See Table 1.)

TABLE 1

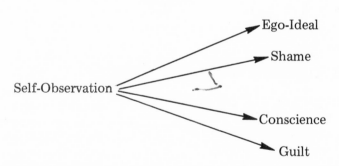

Within this superego construct we deal with shame where we fail to fulfill the demands of the ego-ideal, i.e., where we fail to be as strong, beautiful, self-possessed, competent, sexually potent, etc., as we feel we should be.

We speak of guilt when we violate our conscience, which urges us not to hurt, cheat, humiliate, disobey, etc., those whom we should love or respect. Hence the German notion of guilt as *"Gewissensbiss,"* which means the bite of conscience.

Self-observation, the third superego function, mediates how we experience either shame or guilt. In the meaning here intended, it includes self-judgment, as well as observation and judgment of others and the total situation, insofar as these affect the behavior of the self. Thus, self-observation, in this extended meaning, determines how far we stray from ego-ideal, or conscience, in fact or fantasy. Such self-observation, as is well known, varies greatly among individuals in strictness and acumen. It appears strong, overfocused, and searching in some; and weak, underfocused, and lax in others. Also—and most important—it can be unhooked, perverted, or bypassed, thereby allowing the individual to evade (more or less) the pain of shame or guilt. This defensive usage (or nonusage) of self-observation accounts for characteristic dynamics and discharge routes of shame and guilt, all serving to attenuate pain.

In (actual or potential) shame, the person typically tries massively to avoid or blot out self-observation: he may literally close his eyes to, or hide from and deny, i.e., make nonexistent, what happened. In (actual or potential) guilt, he typically tries to silence the voice of conscience via distortive perception and judgment of accountability, particularly through the use of projection. He may get rid of guilt, at least momentarily, by accusing, blaming, or punishing others; this has been described in the analytical writings of Freud (1926), Fenichel (1945, 1954), and many others. At the same time, he frequently, though unwittingly, sets himself up for being blamed or punished, or embarks on repair work.

HITLER TORN BETWEEN SHAME AND PRIDE

With the above in mind, let us, first, consider how Hitler displayed the dynamics of shame. Clearly, he showed these in almost everything he did or wrote, as he railed continually against what, in his scheme of things, smacked of weakness or defeat, and hence of humiliation: military and political weakness, physical and racial deficiency, effeminacy, halfheartedness, any readiness to compromise or to be swayed by propaganda or sentimentality, ineptitude of all kinds, and perhaps most important, any compassion, tenderness, emotional warmth, playfulness, wholehearted humor—in fact, any spontaneity. For example, Fest (1974) states that "he was good at portraying feelings; he took pains not to show them. He repressed all spontaneity"[6] —and hated, for example, to be seen while playing with one of his dogs. As soon as he knew he was being observed, he coldly chased the dog away. "He was constantly tormented by a fear of seeming ridiculous or of making a *faux pas* that would cause him to forfeit the respect of members of his entourage, down to his janitor. Before he ventured to appear in public in a new suit or a new hat, he would have himself photographed so that he could check the effect. He did not swim, never got into a rowboat . . . or mounted a horse. . . . "[7] and shunned all extravagancies *(Mätzchen)*. "He regarded life as a kind of permanent parade before a gigantic audience . . . he constantly observed himself and literally never spoke an unconsidered word. . . . His desires were secret, his feelings hidden, and the widespread notion of an emotionally ungoverned, wildly gesticulating Hitler actually reverses the proportion of rule and exception. In fact his was the most concentrated life imaginable, disciplined to the point of unnatural rigidity."[8] He was, in brief, haunted by the ever present threat of shame over being or appearing defeated, weak, inept, deficient, inferior.

No doubt, real shame hit him repeatedly with full force. There was, for example, the burning humiliation of the would-be artist of Viennese days who, rebuffed by the Academy of Fine Arts, was reduced to hawking post cards and living among society's dregs. His very passivity, inertia, and anonymity at that time augmented, as well as reflected, his deep shame, as they gave further proof of his weakness, ineptitude, and awkwardness—attributes he loathed. And there was, of course, most shameful of all, Germany's defeat and humiliation in 1918 and later, with which he identified so strongly. No wonder, then, that Hitler furiously tried to wipe out such shame by extolling or practicing what seemed to negate it—a "crystallic hardness," brute strength, superiority, elitism, the need to be in control throughout, to push the most radical solutions to problems, and never to show compassion or pity.

Thus, Hitler appeared hopelessly torn between, on the one side, an unduly harsh and rigid ego-ideal and, on the other, an ego desperately trying to live up to this ideal, yet always falling short. To be sure, he was successful beyond expectations in—seemingly—wiping out earlier humiliations, striding from triumph to ever greater triumphs. And there can be no doubt that he rejoiced in these triumphs, as when he indulged in exorbitant victory celebrations. Yet all these triumphs were short-lived. After a brief respite he again began to crave heroic feats of victory and conquest, and the demands of his ego-ideal grew rather than lessened. He seemed caught in an expanding shame-pride spiral.

One reason Hitler could not escape this spiral was, I believe, his lack of genuine humor and playfulness. Normally, these capacities allow us to deflate a too-rigid and too-serious ego-ideal and thereby to attenuate shame. For Hitler, this would have implied an ability to laugh about himself—to accept his own as well as other people's foibles, to enjoy paradox and whimsy—that he evidently did not possess. But it was not only the lack of such a playful streak that kept him locked into increasingly futile attempts to drown shame in pride and triumph; also contributing to this desperate quest was, I submit, an ever growing sense of (largely unconscious) guilt. Let us, then, look at how this affected him.

GUILT AS A DYNAMIC FORCE IN HITLER

While we can easily spot the dynamics of shame in Hitler, the dynamics of his guilt may elude us. For up to the end he denied he felt guilty about those things which others viewed as horrendous crimes, particularly the killing of the Jews, and his plunging the world into war. Regarding the Jews, he said, at a time when the extermination machinery was running at full speed: "I have had a pure conscience."[9] And regarding the war, he maintained (publicly) to the end—as his political testament, laid down only hours before his death, attests—that he never desired it, always tried to forestall it, and, when it was finally forced upon him, waged it solely in Germany's interests.

Such a steadfast denial of guilt is indeed remarkable. It has caused observers, psychoanalysts among them, to assert that Hitler was devoid of ordinary guilt and that he was either a monstrous narcissist, a defective sociopath, or both. I believe, however, that here again matters are more complex than observers have thus far suspected. For we can neither dismiss Hitler's denials of guilt as mere self-serving ploys, nor fail to notice in him those well-known deeper mechanisms by which individuals try to defend themselves against the anguish and pain of guilt, as mentioned earlier. Let us consider the latter first.

Here, we have seen, the role of distorted as well as distorting self-observation becomes central. Self-observation, we noted, can be unhooked, perverted, or bypassed so that the subject's conscience appears appeased, muted, or blinded, yet remains formidably exacting, albeit in often devious and invisible ways. This happens, typically, in the projective mechanism, described by Freud and others, in which an individual attributes his own guilt-producing traits and motives to others, whom he then blames and attacks. This, we know, Hitler did constantly and massively. As one of countless examples, we may select here the speech he made on July 13, 1934, approximately two weeks after the "Night of the Long Knives" (during which he had hundreds of his alleged opponents killed). In that speech he branded his recently destroyed one-time cronies as conspirators, thereby revealing as well as disowning his *own* conspiratorial motivations.

The first group consists of a small body of international disintegrators, apostles of the world view of Communism, who systematically incite the peoples, break up established order, and endeavor to produce chaos. We seek evidence of the work of these international conspirators everywhere around us, in street fights, war at the barricades, mass terrorism, the individualistic propaganda of disintegration, which disturbs nearly every country of the world. . . .

The second group consists of discontented political leaders. . . . The more time veils with the gracious mantle of forgetfulness their own incapacity, the more do they think themselves entitled gradually to bring themselves back into the people's memory. But since their incapacity was not formerly limited to any special period, but was born in them by nature, they are today unable to prove their value in any positive and useful work, but they see the fulfillment of their life's task in criticism as treacherous as it is mendacious.

The third group of destructive agents is formed of those revolutionaries whose former relation to the state was shattered by the events of 1918; they became uprooted and thereby lost altogether all sympathy with any ordered human society. They became revolutionaries who favored revolution for its own sake and desired to see revolution established as a permanent condition. . . . Among the numberless documents which during the last week it was my duty to read, I have discovered a diary with the notes of a man who, in 1918, was thrown into the path of resistance to the laws and who now lives in the world in which law itself seems to be a provocation to resistance. It is an unnerving document—an unbroken tale of conspiracy and continual plotting. It gives one an insight into the mentality of men who, without realizing it, have found in nihilism their final confession of faith. Incapable of any true cooperation, with a desire to oppose all order, filled with hatred against every authority, their unrest and disquietude can find satisfaction only in some conspiratorial activity of the mind perpetually plotting the disintegration of whatever at any moment exists. . . . This third group of pathological enemies of the state is dangerous because they represent a reservoir of those ready to cooperate in every attempt at a revolt, at least just for so long as a new order does not begin to crystallize out of the state of chaotic confusion.

The fourth group sometimes carries on its destructive activities even against its own will. This group is composed of those persons who belong to a comparatively small section of society and who, having nothing to do, find time and opportunity to report orally everything that has happened in order thus to bring some interesting and important variety into their otherwise completely purposeless lives. . . . Since these men as a result of doing nothing do not possess any living relation to the millions who form the mass of the nation. . . . These people are dangerous because they are move. . . . Because their egos are full of nothingness, and since they find a similar nothingness among their like, they look upon the whole world as equally empty. . . . Their anxieties, they imagine, form the cares of the whole nation. . . . These people are dangerous because they are veritable bacillus-carriers of unrest and uncertainty, of rumors, assertions, lies and suspicions, slanders and fears, and thus they contribute to produce gradually a state of nervousness which spreads among the people, so that in the end it is hard to find or recognize where its influence stops.[10]

But Hitler's distortive self-observation implied more than projection, as it fed on his feats as politician, stagecrafter, and salesman of myths. As politician and possessor of the "stronger reality,"[11] he could make his projections come true by using mass terror and violence; he could force opponents into submission, destroy the underpinnings of their identity and dignity, and make them into grotesque caricatures of their former selves, and could annihilate millions of unwilling victims who failed to fit into what he deemed the right order of things. As political stagecrafter, he could impede and sidetrack self-observation by ever more dazzling displays; and as salesman of myths, he could effectively promote a perspective that lent credence to his own, as well as other people's, distortions.

All this suggests to me that Hitler hated and destroyed not because of a lack, but because of an excess, of (unconscious) guilt, that he vainly tried to escape the pain of guilt by committing more crimes. In other words, I find him trapped in an expanding guilt, as well as shame, spiral.

To understand more clearly what this involved, we must consider one further aspect in the working of shame and guilt.

SHAME-GUILT CYCLES

To my knowledge, the psychoanalyst F. Alexander (1963) was first to describe this aspect. Subsequently, other authors[1][2] elaborated it. I have in mind so-called *shame-guilt* or *guilt-shame cycles*, in which shame and guilt interweave with each other sequentially so as to form alternating elements in one transactional chain. These cycles reflect shifting transactional scenarios and shifting perceptions of meaning and accountability, reminding us of the words of Nietzsche: "There are no moral"—i.e., shame- or guilt-arousing—"phenomena. There is only a moral interpretation of phenomena."[1][3] Dostoevski illustrated complex shame-guilt cycles in his novels; Alexander found them to underlie many criminal careers, as he wrote:

> In the little boy the intensely ambitious and competitive hostile attitude toward brothers and father provokes guilt feelings and fear of retaliation. Under the pressure of guilt feelings and fear he abandons his competitive attitude and adopts a submissive role by means of which the inhibited boy tries to gain the love of his dangerous and powerful competitors. This submissive attitude now creates intense inferiority feelings, hurts the male pride, and leads to aggressive criminal behavior by means of which a tough, independent, stubborn, unyielding attitude is demonstrated and every dependence denied. This attitude becomes a new source of guilt feelings that lead to new inhibitions which again cause inferiority feelings and again stimulate aggressive behavior.[1][4]

Similar cycles are known from psychoanalytic practice. The following cycle, observed in my practice, seems fairly typical: A patient believed he had seriously hurt me by bad-mouthing me to a friend. Stung by guilt, he scrutinized me for evidence that would retrospectively justify his bad-mouthing. He finally focused on my occasional drift into inattention and accused me of not caring for him. When I interpreted his attacks on me as attempts to assuage his guilt over bad-mouthing me, he became upset and cried. Yet while he cried, he was overcome by shame. He called his crying a despicable show of weakness, and blamed me for having triggered it. Out of his humiliated fury, he attacked me again, thus starting a new (albeit slightly attenuated) guilt-shame cycle. (Conceivably, he could also have felt pride over his very weakness and self-disdain. For the possibilities of subjectively juggling meaning and accountability are nearly endless. Nietzsche was aware of this when he wrote: "He who despises himself, still esteems himself as the despiser."[15] And: "We may train our conscience so that it kisses at the same time as it bites.")[16]

HITLER CAUGHT IN SPIRALLING SHAME-GUILT CYCLES

In light of the above, Hitler appears caught up in typically spiralling and inescapable shame-guilt or guilt-shame cycles, albeit ones with unique features. Like the delinquent boy in Franz Alexander's description, to wipe out shame he had to prove his strength and hardness more and more fiercely, which meant he had to commit crimes on an ever larger scale. To justify these crimes—i.e., to avoid the pain of guilt—he had to more and more strenuously distort self-observation; yet to avoid a psychotic break, he also had to revamp reality to let it match such distortion. This, however, became difficult as time went by, as reality became more unyielding and his enemies more powerful. At that point, to avoid a show of weakness, he had to become ever more stubbornly resistent even though doing so sped his destruction. Thus, whatever other suicidal forces operated in Hitler, they now combined with those inherent in the above process.

FAMILIAL SOURCES OF SHAME AND GUILT

If shame and guilt are central to Hitler's destructive dynamics, what are their developmental sources? To answer this question, we must once more look at his early relationships.

Shame, we saw, grows mainly out of competitive defeat, rebuff, and weakness, out of a sensed loss of self-control and self-esteem, and is often specific to a sense of physical and sexual deficiency. Here Hitler's childhood offers us, indeed, several leads that psychoanalytic authors have pursued (without, however, necessarily relating them to shame). There was, first, his monorchism, with its implied sense of sexual deficiency, which Bromberg (1971, 1974) subsequently linked to such compensatory phallic ploys as Hitler's use of his body as phallus, or of his two eyes (i.e., two testicles pushed upward) as castrating weapons. There was, second, very likely, a readiness to identify with his overly close and indulging mother and thus to acquire a basic feminine identification, or latent homosexuality, with strong passive longings—i.e., longings to be dominated or even attacked—which, on a more conscious level, he found shameful and had to repudiate by heroic masculine feats. W. Langer (1972) and J. Brosse (1972), for example, suggested such dynamics. And there was, third, it appears, an interference with young Adolf's self-control when Klara anxiously over-controlled him. For, as Erikson (1968) showed, "A sense of self-control without loss of self-esteem is the ontogenetic source of a sense of free will. From an unavoidable sense of loss of self-control and of parental over-control comes a lasting propensity for doubt and shame."[1][7] And such a "lasting propensity for doubt and shame," instilled at a formative early period, may well have fatefully shaped Hitler's life.

Hitler's (assumed) guilt, we saw earlier, has been viewed mainly in an oedipal context, as most analytic authors have dwelt on his incestuous wishes for his mother and/or death wishes for his father. (Some authors, such as Fromm and Brosse, found his death wishes to be aimed at both parents.) If we take Hitler's "*Weltanschauung*" and major projections as our guide here, guilt associated with incestuous and patricidal motives seemed, indeed, pervasive, as Hitler railed continually against the mixing of the Aryan and Jewish races (something which G. Kurth [1947, 1950], for one, traced to Hitler's own incestuous wishes and fears) and against Germany's ruthlessly scheming enemies.

But such traditional views on the sources of shame and guilt in Hitler's psychology, I submit, are insufficient. Specifically, they fail to illuminate crucial transactional—or systems—aspects of shame and guilt. To get hold of these aspects, a further consideration of the binding and delegating dynamics outlined in Chapter II is needed. In these dynamics, we found guilt over betrayal of loyalty—particularly breakaway guilt and guilt over failing in one's missions—to be central. Here I shall further elaborate this centrality by linking it to the ideas advanced in this chapter. To do so, I must first briefly review some traditional psychoanalytic notions regarding a child's superego development.

PARENTAL CONTRIBUTIONS TO THE
CHILD'S SUPEREGO DEVELOPMENT

To conceptualize and understand a child's superego development (and hence his later bouts with shame and guilt), psychoanalytic theory focused chiefly on the vicissitudes of identification. The works of S. Freud (particularly on the oedipus complex [1905]), A. Freud (1946), and many others established this perspective. H. B. Lewis (1971), summarizing the major work in this area, distinguished between two prototypes of identification that may tilt superego development in the direction of either shame or guilt proneness. In the first type, called "anaclitic identification," the child, destined to become shame-prone, internalizes the parental ego-ideal primarily in the context of a dependent, submissive, and admiring relationship. In the second type, he identifies with the aggressor, as described by A. Freud (1946). Here his submissiveness becomes ambivalently tainted with retaliatory, albeit subdued, aggression. Given a sufficient capacity for concern (in Winnicott's meaning of the term), such a child will very likely feel the bite of conscience acutely and be primarily guilt-prone.

However, these and similar efforts to conceptualize superego formation from the vantage point of the identifying (or internalizing) child remain limited. We must integrate them with a family perspective which recognizes the contributions of parents *and* children. And it is this family perspective which, I believe, my concept of binding and delegating processes provides.

Let us, then, with our present focus on shame and guilt, take a new look at those missions in which delegates primarily serve their parents' ego-ideal, conscience, and self-observation.

Where a delegate must chiefly fulfill a parent's unrealized ego-ideal, i.e., must turn into the creative writer, artist, actor, scientist, or business tycoon that the parent failed to become, he becomes vital to his parent's pride-shame regulation primarily: in embodying their extended ego-ideal, it is now up to him to save them from being crushed by their chronic and seemingly irremediable shame.

Where delegates primarily serve their parents' conscience, guilt rather than shame is at issue. Winnicott (1958), for one, referred to children who seem weighed down and made joyless by what we may call "borrowed guilt," i.e., guilt borrowed from their parents. He noted that a child's "reparation urge may be related less to the personal guilt-sense than to the guilt-sense or depressed mood of a parent."[18] A borrowing of guilt on the children's part, however, implies a lending, or trading, of it on the part of their parents, as can be seen in the previously mentioned example of the German students who worked in Israeli kibbutzim to atone for a guilt that their parents, one-time supporters of Nazi Germany, had incurred yet disowned. Efforts to undo parental guilt by proxy may be no less exacting than those to undo chronic parental shame. Such delegates, we saw further, in addition to doing their parents' repair work, frequently become targets for their parents' wrath. They must then let themselves be victimized and thereby must whitewash their parents' conscience—i.e., must act so provocatively as to justify their parents' attacks on them. They may remind us then of those loyal Communists, described in A. Koestler's *Darkness at Noon* (1941) who, even though innocent, confessed to heinous anti-Communist crimes, thereby destroying themselves while vindicating Stalin, their delegator.

Delegates, finally, who serve their parents' ego-ideal or conscience and thereby relieve them of shame or guilt also serve their parents' self-observation; or more correctly, *serve their distortive use of self-observation.* Through their actions they now substantiate, at least partially, their parents' misperceptions and misjudgments regarding the sources of, and accountability for, the shame and guilt at issue. Thus, such self-observation is no longer distorted as, in Hegel's words, "the negation is negated." The parents can now easily shame their children for their own disowned weakness, ineptitude, messiness, etc., and can make them feel guilty for their own disowned badness, rebellion, or neglect. The child is not only made to fit, but also fits himself into the parents' extended self, an ever accessible container for their disowned, yet potentially most painful, experiences—those involving shame and guilt.

HITLER'S MISSIONS RECONSIDERED

In earlier describing Hitler as Klara's delegate, I delineated four major missions: to absorb her regressive gratification and, in so doing, nurture her; to redeem her worth as mother; to provide her with vicarious power and importance; and, finally, to avenge her. All these missions, we find now, served Klara's ego-ideal (i.e., her shame-pride regulation), her conscience (i.e., served to appease *her* unconscious guilt), and also her distorted self-observation.

To appreciate the first function—to relieve his mother's shame—we must recall her lowly and captive housewife status, so well described by Smith (1967). Here the outward demeanor of the ever submissive, ever respectful, uneducated, and church-abiding young wife conveyed a vulnerability to the deepest shame, just as that of her husband, so it appears, conveyed imperviousness and pride. Thus I believe Hitler, bound to her as her delegate, could not help suffering *her* shame just as in 1918 he suffered Germany's (his new mother's) shame, which he then tried to wipe out in torrents of triumph.

To assess the second superego function—to serve Klara's conscience (i.e., to appease her guilt)—we must recall how she, as a lodger and maid in her "uncle's" house, had an (almost) incestuous affair with him while his legitimate wife was still alive. Here I agree with Binion that to lose her first three children in rapid succession may well have signaled to her God's punishment and wrath, particularly since her stepchildren survived. To relieve his mother's guilt here, Hitler primarily had to confirm her as a nurturant and nondestructive mother. In so doing, he sucked in with his mother's milk not only her trauma (the deaths of her children), as Binion suggests,[19] but also, I believe, her gnawing guilt over having invited this trauma. And, to the extent that she commissioned Adolf as her avenger, here again she foisted on him guilt for wishes and acts that she herself, very likely, disowned to the end.

To make a final assessment of the third function—to serve her distorted self-observation—we would, indeed, have to know more than we do and, most inportant, would have to glean the subtle quality of her mainly nonverbal communications with Adolf. But if clinical experience is any guide, we can assume that, to a large extent at least, her conflictful messages and shared fantasies fed his later *"Weltanschauung,"* a *Weltanschauung* that—primitive, absurd, convincing, and coherent at one and the same time—then defined meaning and juggled accountability for him in accord with *her* wishes and visions.

PSYCHOLOGICAL EXPLOITATION
AND COUNTEREXPLOITATION

Once we take into account how parents abet their children's conflicts and plights, we confront a momentous drama. Psychological exploitation and counterexploitation; an immense, though thwarted, need for repair work, as well as for revenge; a deeply felt sense of justice or injustice committed, and of loyalty confirmed or betrayed—all of these, operating largely without awareness, become formidable dynamic forces, influencing the members' every move. And the stakes in this "morality play" are high. On the one side we find parents who, exploited and crippled by their own parents, attempt to survive by living through their children, crippling them in turn, as they subject them to "missions impossible." On the other side, we find children who, while they labor under such missions, may excel in heroism, sacrifice, or both.

Unfortunately, with Hitler we cannot observe this drama as in family therapies, where the members' exploitative and counterexploitative moves unfold before our eyes and can be discussed and clarified. Rather, we must now reconstruct it from sparse, indirect, and possibly misleading evidence. Still, I believe, we can glean at least the outline of a plot in which Hitler, as his mother's bound delegate, was at one and the same time extraordinarily favored and disfavored, privileged and burdened.

He was favored because he received both her nearly exclusive love and, as a being vital to her own psychological survival, a sense of being uniquely important, powerful, and chosen, "gifts" without which he could have never achieved what he did.

At the same time, he was massively exploited and deprived. Specifically, he was from the outset burdened with shame and guilt that were not of his making. Thus he became subject to an uneven psychological differentiation and integration, because he had to channel his energies and skills into fulfilling nearly unfulfillable missions and into resolving nearly unresolvable conflicts. This, I believe, largely accounts for the contrast between, on the one hand, Hitler the formidably complex and talented genius and, on the other, Hitler the pathetically neurotic, banal, and morally defective nonperson (Unperson) whom Fest, among other biographers, has portrayed. I, for one, find here a massive stunting of growth that derived from, and also sustained, an extraordinarily uneven development.

Given the above ambiguity in Hitler's "ledger of merits,"[20] it need not surprise us that he seemed devoid of, as well as consumed by, guilt. For he could flaunt his good conscience as long as he viewed himself, within *his* scheme of justice, as having fulfilled his part of the bargain. Hence Hitler, most likely, believed what he wrote in his last testament only hours before his suicide, notwithstanding the contradictory evidence contained in many of his other statements, both spoken and written:

My Political Testament

Since 1914 when, as a volunteer, I made my modest contribution in the World War which was forced upon the Reich, over thirty years have passed.

In these three decades only love for my people and loyalty to my people have guided me in all my thoughts, actions, and life. They gave me the strength to make the most difficult decisions, such as no mortal has yet had to face. I have exhausted my time, my working energy, and my health in these three decades.

It is untrue that I or anybody else in Germany wanted war in 1939. It was desired and instigated exclusively by those international statesmen who were either of Jewish origin or working for Jewish interests. I have made so many offers for the reduction and limitation of armaments, which posterity cannot explain away for all eternity, that the responsibility for the outbreak of this war cannot rest on me. Furthermore, I never desired that after the first terrible World War a second war should arise against England or even against America. Centuries may pass, but out of the ruins of our cities and monuments of art there will arise anew the hatred for the people who alone are ultimately responsible: international Jewry and its helpers!

As late as three days before the outbreak of the German-Polish war, I proposed to the British Ambassador in Berlin a solution of the German-Polish problem—similar to the problem of the Saar area, under international control. This offer cannot be explained away, either. It was only rejected because the responsible circles in English politics wanted the war, partly in the expectation of business advantages, partly driven by propaganda promoted by international Jewry.

But I left no doubt about the fact that if the peoples of Europe were again to be treated as so many packages of shares by these international money and finance conspirators, then the people who bear the real guilt for this murderous struggle would also have to answer for it: the Jews! It also left no doubt that this time we would not permit millions of European children of Aryan descent to die of hunger, or millions of grown-up men to suffer death, or hundreds of thousands of women and children to be burned and bombed to death in the cities, without the real culprit suffering his due punishment, though in a more humane way."[2] [1]

Here I see Hitler behaving like those modern-day guerrilla fighters and highjackers who—bursting with rage over disputable, yet (by them) deeply believed, injustices—readily commit what to others seem horrendous crimes, even though, and because, they perish committing them. For, in their own balance sheet, they come out guilt-free, as their past sufferings, the nobility of their purpose, and their personal sacrifice outweigh all the harm they may cause others.

THE DYNAMICS OF VENGEFULNESS,
FELT INJUSTICE, AND HIDDEN LOYALTY

This, then, forces us to take another look at Hitler's extraordinary vengefulness, which figures so centrally in his destructiveness and radicalism. For, contrary to what Fromm and others allege, this vengefulness gives evidence of an intense, albeit invisible and conflicted, loyalty rather than of massive alienation. The psychoanalyst H. Searles (1959), for one, has shown that vengefulness stems from early symbiotic (or, if you wish, bound-up) relationships in which the child suffers massive frustration and separation-anxiety and defends against grief. In my clinical experience, I have found that it also derives from a deep sense of injustice, originally experienced within early binding relationships, but now enacted with other persons or the world at large. Through such displacement the primary loyalty bond is safeguarded, while others bear the brunt of one's vengeful rage. This typically happens, for example, with the spouse who brutally rails against the other spouse yet, at the same time, avoids experiencing or examining the loyalty *and* sense of unjust treatment he or she (unconsciously) felt and still feels toward a parent (or parents), a process which I. Boszormenyi-Nagy (1972) has well described.

If Hitler was, as I suggest, burdened with his mother's disowned shame and guilt, was entrusted with "missions impossible," was subjected to unbearable conflicts, and hence was psychologically exploited and stunted in his growth, he indeed had reason to feel unjustly treated, as his slate had been negatively loaded from the start. But insofar as he also loved and needed his mother, he could not afford to pay her back directly. Rather, he had to displace his retaliatory fury onto others and eventually onto the whole non-German world, thereby compounding a millionfold the injustice he had suffered, but keeping the original loyalty bond intact and unquestioned.

With the above in mind, let us once more consider how Hitler portrayed the Jews, his chief enemies. Monotonously he called them schemers, parasites, profiteers, poisoners, traitors, and exploiters who lacked integrity. Clearly such a portrait reveals his projections; but beyond that, I believe, it reveals a burning rage over what once happened to him—his own exploitation, "poisoning," and unfair treatments; in other words, it reveals an attempt to seek restitutive, yet displaced, justice.

Binion, we saw earlier, viewed a Jewish doctor as (next to Hitler's mother) the central person in Hitler's drama of hidden revenge and loyalty, as it was Dr. Bloch who, from Adolf's unconscious point of view, poisoned her and profited from her death. Yet in light of the above, Bloch's role becomes less central, for he now figures chiefly as a stand-in for the more important *dramatis personae:* Hitler's parents. Of these, his father Alois, as we saw earlier, almost certainly exemplified a lack of fairness, integrity, true authority, and loyalty in his treatment of wife and children (and possibly in his official acts as well). We also find in Hitler's halfbrother, Alois, Jr., a ne'er-do-well and "sociopath," evidence of Alois, Sr.'s failure as a loving, integral, and limit-setting father; indeed, the brother—an "irresponsible, wayward expellee"—suggests paternal rejection and neglect almost more than Adolf himself. But apparently even more important here were his mother's contributions, i.e., *her* lack of fairness and *her* exploitation of Adolf, an exploitation inherent in her very self-sacrificing overdevotion, because this caused in him an unresolvable, albeit subtle and ambiguous, indebtedness.

These last were contributions Hitler had to dissociate most deeply from his awareness, requiring a displacement of retaliatory fury so gigantic that millions of innocents fell victim to it. Still, as time went by even this massive dissociation seemed threatened. For as the tides of war turned, Hitler's once blissful, reciprocally nurturing symbiosis with Germany became strained and the vengefulness he had so far displaced onto Germany's enemies now increasingly fell upon Germany herself. "If the German people are not ready to fight for their survival (*Selbstbehauptung*), well, then they have to disappear (*dann soll es verschwinden*)," we hear him say as early as January 1942.[22] And as his own and Germany's defeat drew nearer, he found traitorous, cowardly, scheming, undignified—i.e., "Jewish"—elements increasingly festering within Germany's very body. In the last weeks of his career, even Himmler (Himmler, "most loyal of the loyal"—*der Treueste der Treuen*, nicknamed also the loyal Henry—*der "treue Heinrich"*) and Goering deserted him, among countless others. And while he thus found the "Jew" corroding Germany's soul ever more ominously, he might conceivably have moved closer to recognizing the Ur-source of most of his perceptions of injustice and rage—his mother and family—yet by no means close enough to truly understand and mourn what had happened.

THE INABILITY TO MOURN

For even though Hitler, according to Dr. Bloch and Kubizek,

looked stricken over his mother's illness and death, he failed to mourn her successfully—if by mourning we mean that process described by Freud that painfully, and bit by bit, makes us reexperience what tied us to the lost object—love, devotion, ambivalence, rage, contempt, and much, much more—and that finally allows us to give it up in fantasy as well as in fact. Rather than thus mourning his mother, Hitler tried to deny her loss and to safeguard her idealized image—at enormous expense, as it turned out, to himself and untold others.[23]

CHAPTER V

HITLER AND HIS FOLLOWERS:
A VIEW ON GROUP DYNAMICS

I shall, in this final chapter, shift the focus of our inquiry and
see Hitler as a link in a wider transactional chain. Rather than see
him as a unique creative "artist," I shall view him here as a catalyst
of longings and (seeming) resolver of the conflicts that countless
Germans shared.

What, then, were these longings and conflicts? To understand
and appreciate them we must now look, if only briefly, at
Germany's history and the Weimar Republic in which Hitler found
his followers.

THE ROAD TO WEIMAR

Germans associate Weimar not only with their ill-fated
experiment in democracy but also with Goethe and Schiller,
German literary heroes who, some two hundred years ago, lived
and worked in the small town and dukedom of that name. And
students of German history, no less than students of Hitler,
confront at once the task of reconciling in their minds these two
Weimars—one an embodiment of cultured humanity, the other a
springboard for Hitler.[1]

Thus, when we look at Germany's past, we need a perspective

that somehow spans these contrasts. And that, I believe, must be one which takes into account a geography that gave Germany few natural boundaries, yet made her Europe's heartland. Such geography, it seems to me, bequeathed to Germany, as to "a delegate of destiny," the mission of developing out of Europe's diverse elements a viable national identity that also sustained a wider cosmopolitan vision. Goethe's and Schiller's Weimar—occupying (nearly) the middle of Germany, just as Germany herself, along with the Swiss confederacy, occupied the middle of Europe—exemplified such a mission of reconciliation. Yet so, in its own way, did Hitler's *Reich*, the third in a series of German *Reiche* that began with Charlemagne, or Charles the Great—*Karl der Grosse*, as the Germans like to call him.

For in 80 A.D. this Carolingian king made Pope Leo III crown him ruler of the "Holy Roman Empire," which was subsequently renamed the "Holy Roman Empire of the German Nation." Thereby Charlemagne introduced a concept that seemed to reconcile the traditions of ancient Rome with the new structures of feudalism, a Mediterranean Christian faith with Northern piousness, and Latin culture with Germanic vitality. The Holy Roman Empire—spanning then a vast territory that encompassed much of present-day France and Germany—lasted, on paper at least, until 1806 when Napoleon, another self-styled emperor, finally dissolved it.

There followed a second *Reich* in 1871, when the German states, victorious in their war against France, united under Prussia's hegemony. This *Reich* ended with Germany's defeat in World War I. The Third *Reich* of Hitler emerged in 1933.

But while her centrality in Europe bequeathed to Germany a task of reconciliation, it also made her vulnerable. Throughout her history, foreign invaders traversed her soil and foreign interests divided the loyalties of her people. Here the Thirty Years War stands out; it decimated Germany's population and left her social, political, and religious fabric in shambles. Also, with so much cross-cultural traffic going on, her borders seemed forever in flux, and imprecise geographic borders implied imprecise linguistic boundaries, blurring in turn the sense of national identity.[2] Thus the Dutch, Flemish, Alsatians, as well as many Swiss and Austrians, spoke German idioms, but for the most part felt little if any allegiance to Germany. But perhaps most important, the notion of a strong, unified, yet reconciling *Reich*—this legacy from Charlemagne's time—was made a travesty by the actual conduct of the German princes who, by and large, felt no bond to a higher German cause and consumed their energies in petty power politics.

It was only in the latter part of the 19th century that Germany, under the guidance of Bismarck, achieved the political strength, unity, and sense of purpose that seemed her due as Europe's heartland. However, even then she remained ill-equipped for the task of reconciliation. For Bismarck, the Prussian junker and *"Iron Kanzler"* (Chancellor), did little, if anything, to strengthen Germany's retarded democratic institutions. Rather, he despised and undermined them. Essentially, he represented an elitist *"Führerprinzip"* that demanded a corresponding *"Untertanengehorsam"* (the obedience of subordinates) and, in effect, made Germany big by making the Germans small.

Still, Bismarck was intelligent and, as architect of Germany's foreign policy, restrained.[3] The Hohenzollern monarch, Wilhelm II, who succeeded him, had neither of these attributes. Driven by a pathetic sense of inferiority and guided by nationalist conservatives, he was outwardly arrogant and full of bombast, turning imperialist with a vengeance, as it were, and he made Germany, a relative latecomer in worldwide power politics, join the Western nations' scramble for colonies and spheres of interest. In so doing, he pushed Germany's military powers to awesome heights and also elicited her neighbors' distrust and fear.

The stage was thus set for that fateful war out of which the Weimar Republic and Hitler's Third *Reich* arose, a war that, after the euphoria brought by early victories, exposed the mass of Germans to ever increasing frustration, hunger, and, finally, humiliation and defeat. And it was in this defeat that, for the first time in her history, full democracy came to Germany.

It could not have come under worse auspices. For there was not only the legacy of the lost war, there was now also, compounding it, the legacy of Bismarck's authoritarianism which predisposed Germans to a jaundiced view of parliamentary democracy. (Thus, Germany's elite continued to shun the "dirty business of politics" and pursued the more prestige-laden careers of academicians, business entrepreneurs, civil servants, and army officers.) And there was, finally, an economy totally out of kilter. Largely as a result of the victors' claims for massive financial reparations, inflation skyrocketed. Eventually, billions of German marks were hardly worth the paper on which they were printed. As a result, millions of Germans, particularly those of the middle class, lost their savings, their social status, their self-respect, and their political bearings.

While this happened, the lure and strength of radical forces—on the right and left of the political spectrum—grew. On the right there were mainly the hordes of frustrated and jobless ex-soldiers who flocked into Hitler's SA and SS; on the left were Communists who tried to import the Russian revolution into Germany. While both sides were at loggerheads with each other—and frequently clashed in bloody street fights—they were united in despising and further undermining Germany's feeble democratic center. Therefore civil war and chaos often seemed around the corner, if not at hand.

Under these circumstances it would have required a near miracle for the Weimar Republic to survive. But it almost did. From 1924 on, the country seemed on the road to economic recovery and a precarious stability. In the middle or late twenties, Hitler's appeal waned and not a few Nazis despaired of seizing power. This changed, however, in November 1929 when on Wall Street the stock market tumbled and a worldwide depression set in. In Germany it led to millions of unemployed and rapidly growing insecurity and frustration that greatly aided Hitler in the struggle for power.

Against this historical background, let us now consider those transpersonal processes and conditions that account for Hitler's impact. Again my objectives are limited: I shall largely bypass many interweaving political and social processes and concentrate on the chiefly psychological ones that my family framework highlights. Among these, group processes appear central. To examine them, let us begin by sketching out Hitler's own view and model of group dynamics, as implied in *Mein Kampf* and elsewhere.

HITLER'S MODEL OF GROUP DYNAMICS

Essentially, Hitler looked at groups not as a theoretician but as a pragmatist, i.e., with a view to influencing them as power technician, stagecrafter, or salesman of myths. This meant that he saw group processes as unfolding primarily between leader and group, and emphasized the leader's contributions. Mostly he thought in terms of a large group or groups: of nations (*Völker*), or huge masses. Of these, of course, the German nation, or *Völk*, and the German masses primarily interested him.

Here, however, Hitler appeared ambivalent. To the extent that he addressed the Germans as nation or *Völk*, they connoted enormous power, had the highest culture, were the superior race, and embodied what is best in man: idealism, dignity, and a spirit of sacrifice. But, to the extent that he viewed them as masses, he judged them contemptuously as unstable, stupid, corrupt, unprincipled, weak, and easily dominated. "The receptivity of the great masses is very limited," he wrote, "their intelligence is small, but their power of forgetting is enormous."[4] Essentially, Hitler voiced here notions developed by the Frenchman le Bon in *The Crowd*, his study of the popular mind. Again, this paradoxical attitude reflects, it appears, a basic ambivalence toward Hitler's primary love object, his mother—now resurrected in Germany—whom he needed to adore and idealize, yet also to castigate and debase.[5]

In handling the German masses (or groups), he therefore, as leader and creative artist, faced the problem of transforming these masses' fickleness into determination, their forgetfulness into conviction, their baser instincts into noble strivings, their submissiveness into power and dominance. Here, the secret of success lay for him in the leader's use of propaganda, the essence of which he summarized as follows:

> Effect on the broad masses, concentration on a few points, constant repetition of the same, self-assured and self-reliant framing of the text in the forms of an apodictic statement, greatest perseverance in distribution, and patience in awaiting the effect.[6]

He considered it crucial here not to dilute the masses' attention but concentrate it on one foe only:

> The more unified the application of a people's will to fight, the greater will be the magnetic attraction of a movement and the mightier will be the impetus of the thrust. It belongs to the genius of a great leader to make even adversaries far removed from one another seem to belong to a single category, because in weak and uncertain characters the knowledge of having different enemies can only too readily lead to the beginning of doubt in their own right.
>
> Once the wavering mass sees itself in a struggle against too many enemies, objectivity will put in an appearance, throwing open the question whether all others are really wrong and only their own people or their own movement are in the right.
>
> And this brings about the first paralysis of their own power.[7]

Here the leader's "indomitable energy and will, and if necessary . . . brutal ruthlessness"[8] become the major elements.

For faith, according to Hitler,

> is harder to shake than knowledge, love succumbs less to change than respect, hate is more enduring than aversion, and the impetus to the mightiest upheavals on this earth has at all times consisted less in a scientific knowledge dominating the masses than in a fanaticism which inspired them and sometimes in a hysteria which drove them forward.[9]

Hence, he concludes:

> From the army of often millions of men . . . *one* man must step forward who with apodictic force will form granite principles from the wavering idea-world of the broad masses and take up the struggle for their sole correctness, until from the shifting waves of a free thought-world there will arise a brazen cliff of solid unity in faith and will.[10]

FREUD'S MODEL OF GROUP PROCESSES

Both group processes, clearly, imply much more than such a transformation of fickle into fanatic masses through a leader's use of propaganda and unifying power. Here Freud provided conceptual tools and opened new perspectives. Among other things, he showed how shame and guilt—so central in Hitler's psychology—relate to phenomena that operate in small as well as large groups (including whole nations or cultures). Freud's concept of the superego and/or ego-ideal is also pivotal to our understanding these phenomena: "The ego-ideal," he wrote, "opens up an important avenue for the understanding of group psychology. In addition to its individual side, this ideal has a social side, it is also the common ideal of a family, a class, or a nation."[11]

In a group, Freud argued, the individual gives up his ego-ideal and substitutes for it the group ideal, embodied by the leader. At the same time he identifies—or, better, overidentifies—with the other group members. According to H. Kohut (1972), he is also frequently bolstered by a shared "grandiose group self." This results, then, in the freeing of normally repressed wishes and in the suspension of the ordinary, i.e., culturally conditioned, workings of shame and guilt. As part of the group, the individual indulges in acts that otherwise would excruciatingly embarrass or pain him. This is one reason why seemingly innocuous German citizens, transformed into members of an SS unit, could murder innocent women and children, and why today suburban businessmen and housewives can, as members of an encounter group, shout obscenities, dance in the nude, or examine each other's genitals with specula. These group dynamics—surrender of the ego-ideal to the group leader and each member's concomitant heightened identification with other members—generate apparent shamelessness or guiltlessness and can turn what normally would be considered abominable or shameful into a source of pride and triumph. Heinrich Himmler's notorious speech before a select group of SS men, explicating Hitler's (his delegator's) sentiments, offers one example of such a transformation of normally shameful and guilt-ridden behavior:

> Among ourselves it should be mentioned quite frankly—but we will never speak of it publicly—just as we did not hestitate on 30 June 1934 to do the duty we were told to do and stand comrades who had lapsed up against the wall and shoot them, so we have never spoken about it and will never speak of this . . . I mean cleaning out the Jews, the extermination of the Jewish race. It is one of those things it's easy to talk about—"The Jewish race is being exterminated . . . it's our programme, and we're doing it." And then they come, eighty million worthy Germans, and each one of them has his decent Jew. Of course the others are vermin, but this particular Jew is a first-rate man. . . . Most of *you* must know what it means when a hundred corpses are lying side by side, or five hundred or a thousand. To have stuck it out and at the same time (apart from exceptions caused by human weakness) to have remained decent fellows, that is what has made us so hard. This is a page of glory in our history which has never been written and will never be written.[1][2]

BION'S MODEL OF GROUP DYNAMICS

Freud's model of group dynamics, like Hitler's, emphasizes the leader's contributions, as it is he who manipulates, if not suspends, the group's ego-ideal. At the same time, Freud's model highlights the group's contributions, i.e., those primitive and regressive wishes, drives, and fantasies that the group process unleashes, amplifies, and utilizes.

W. Bion (1948, 1952, 1959) extended and modified this model. Specifically, he described how certain groups organize and operate as if directed by typical, shared fantasies, or, as he called them, "basic assumptions." He contrasted these "basic assumption groups" with "work groups," and he elaborated their differences. In basic assumption groups, the members have little or no sense of collective responsibility and expect to be led. They shun external reality as much as they can. "All coldness is outside; all warmth is inside, with members huddling together like so many babes in the wood . . . outside is death; inside is life."[13] The group climate exerts a regressive pull. Increasingly, the members share a (spurious) sense of omnipotency, remember poorly, and therefore lack a sense of temporal sequences and realistic constraints. If they think at all, they do so in global, simplistic, and wishful ways and seem unable to use their former experiences and skills.

Essentially, Bion distinguished three types of groups, depending on which basic assumption predominates at any given moment: the *basic assumption dependency group*, the *basic assumption fight/flight group*, and the *basic assumption pairing group*. P. Turquet (1974), a student of Bion, added to these a fourth—the *basic assumption oneness group*.

In the dependency group, the members want, above all, security and emotional nurturance. In the fight/flight group, they need to fight or fly from somebody or something. In the pairing group, they strive to create something, some hope, some new idea or Messiah through a pair that is recruited *from*, and—to use my concept—delegated *by* the group. In the oneness group, they "seek to join in a powerful union with an omnipotent force, unobtainably high, to surrender self for passive participation, and thereby to feel existence, well-being and wholeness."[14] Bion (1961) and Turquet (1965, 1971, 1974) provide ample examples from their experiences with such groups.

When the focus is on these basic assumptions, the leader's contributions lose, and those of the group gain, in relative importance; in a sense, the group makes him its patsy. Where, for example, the basic assumption *"dependency"* reigns, the leader is willy-nilly held capable of giving what the group intensely, albeit dimly, craves: security and regressive gratification of primitive, inordinate wishes. The group, accordingly, is passively expectant, hanging on his words, patiently—but also ominously—waiting. To survive, the leader must fit himself to the basic assumption, i.e., must—somehow, some way—deliver what the group expects, or must at least uphold the promise that he can and will do so. Where, on the other hand, the basic assumption *"fight/flight"* predominates, the group channels onto him its (fantasy-inspired) need to fight or to flee an enemy, and he must constitute or supply such. Again his survival as group leader depends on how he responds. Where the basic assumption *"pairing"* prevails, he must nourish, as well as respond to, the shared fantasy that out of two group members'—eagerly watched—intimacy, a savior, and with him a new beginning, will come forth. Where, finally, the basic assumption *"oneness"* takes hold, the group deifies its leader, who now must convincingly impersonate God.

Since Bion and Turquet reported these ideas and observations, they have given rise to a sophisticated literature on group processes and fantasies.[15] L. deMause summarizes some of its tenets, as follows:

> ... the group believes it exists for the purpose of preserving the group ... Groups need leaders to be receptacles for bad internal objects ... these leaders are then deified in order to sustain fantasies of nurturance, and to defend group members against persecutory hostility thought to reside in the group ... also, deification of leaders is a group defense against powerful feelings of abandonment, and ... when this deification decays, revolutionary attempts and an upsurge of group solidarity and utopian fantasies invariably follow ... sub-groups arise from shared defensive styles (i.e., shared basic assumptions) rather than differing needs ... group roles are always collaborative, with leaders, heroes, scapegoats, moralists, and paranoid spokesmen invariably arising to satisfy group needs ... the larger the group the more it is a receptable for repressed feelings, and the more often splitting is used to control projected group violence.[16]

These tenets build, above all, on ideas of M. Klein (1946, 1957), the noted child analyst who influenced Bion as well as other group theorists. According to this author, even a young child has an intense fantasy life that reflects, as well as shapes, primitive intrapsychic conflicts and defenses. Mostly, these center around his (assumed) primitive envy and destructiveness. The child, unable to "own" such envy and destructiveness, disowns them by splitting them off and projecting them into the mother or the maternal breast. These are also called the child's early object, or part object respectively. But since he depends on his mother (or her breast), these disowned elements return to him with a vengeance. They turn the mother and her breast into frightening, persecutory forces which embroil him now in deepest interpersonal conflict, from which there is no respite. It is then this drama of primitive ambivalence, of (essentially) futile attempts at obtaining infantile bliss and at disowning—i.e., splitting off and projecting—infantile drives and anxieties that the above group process mirrors or reenacts.

Institutions, too—the church, the army, the government, the school, etc.—appear to mirror as well as reenact such infantile group fantasies, e.g., the church, group fantasies of dependency; the army, group fantasies of rage; government, group fantasies of omnipotence; the school, group fantasies of control.

Finally, we observe such group fantasies to operate in religious and ideological movements, in that these often represent early infantile part objects.[17] Frequently the imagery of these part objects implies primitive, i.e., preoedipal, ambivalence or denial. Thus, the church stands for the good, flowing breast, the virgin for the unbloody vagina, the witch for the bad, poisonous breast, Christ for the killed yet living son, God for the infanticidal yet divine Father, the "Capitalist" (to the Communist) for the exploitative, controlling mother, the "Communist" (to the capitalist) for the raging baby.

No doubt, these ideas can throw light on Hitler's relations with Germany. For, like Freud's group theory, they provide conceptual tools to grasp the fit between Hitler's and the German people's contributions. For example, in this framework Hitler's "unerring certainty and power of will" matches a group expectancy (or fantasy) of dependency and oneness, his hammering away at the Jews matches one of "fight/flight" (i.e., serves to "split off" and control the group's projected violence), and his pose of God-like omnipotence matches the group's underlying fear of abandonment.

But while group theories such as those I have outlined can account for important features in Hitler's relations with the German people, they need, I believe, to be reconciled with another kind of group theory—one that involves a family concept. To understand this, we must remind ourselves that Bion gleaned his model chiefly from transient groups, i.e., ad hoc aggregates of people who lacked a common history and who, apart from the immediate group relationship, were not mutually involved. Where Bion and other group theorists theorized on nontransient groups such as the army or church, they mainly extrapolated from what they observed in ad hoc groups. (Transiency remains even today the chief criterion for those Bion groups which operate in large parts of the Western world—either as laboratories for the participatory study of small group behavior, or for therapeutic purposes.)

The German people, in contrast, formed a very large nontransient group: its members were mutually involved, and shared a common history and fate—two facts that staked out leader-group relations differing from those that Bion and his followers primarily observed, and that made the Germans as a group more akin to a family.

Where a group is large, a leader must, above all, counteract its ever-present tendency to chaotic fragmentation of wills, amorphousness, and paralysis of action. To do so, he must provide meaning, structure, and purpose, and must unify the individual wills in one common will. This he can do more easily the less he deals with an ad hoc group and the more he can play on the group's common culture, history, and fate, i.e., can appeal to it as *Völk*, nation, or family group. Hitler, we know, did just that to the utmost, the more so as he constantly promoted the one kind of shared group experience most likely to mold a large group into one *"Schicksalsgemeinschaft"* or super-family: a jointly fought war.

This implied, then, that he elicited, as well as responded to, group experiences of at least two kinds: one that grew out of the group's regressive pull and denoted primitive greed, aggression, and infantile feelings of abandonment and other normally censored emotions, as well as volatility of moods, a shared sense of omnipotency, and a lack of either realistic time perspectives or of responsible accounting (an experience that resonated with Hitler's view of the German people as fickle, corrupt masses); and another that grew out of the group's shared efforts, history, and fate, out of what the group members had suffered together, and what they had done or not done to each other—one that grew, as it were, out of the factuality of their joint—past, present, or future—existence, an experience that resonated with Hitler's view of the German people as a noble *Schicksalsgemeinschaft*.

Both kinds of group experiences, we find at closer inspection, imply defensive mechanisms that distort self-observation on the group level. For in both, the members shun an unpleasant reality, as they would otherwise suffer terror, disintegration, and chaos. But—and this seems important here—these defensive mechanisms differ in the two experiences, and therefore structure differently the interactions between the group and its leader.

In the first experience we find the group's defense to rely

essentially on fantasies of the Bion type, described earlier, fantasies that grow out of, and defend the members against, the ambivalence and conflicts that arise along with the primitive needs and drives that the group process in such ad hoc groups unleashes, yet cannot fulfill—except, that is, in fantasy.

In the second experience, we find the defense to rely essentially on what I—in contradistinction to the above group fantasies—would describe as *group or family myths*. These myths I find typically operative in groups whose members share a common past, are factually and fatefully entangled, and which thereby come to resemble actual families, regardless of the group's size. For example, I observed such myths in a closely knit group of medical practitioners whom I once—after the model of so-called Balint groups—lectured and supervised. While the members struggled to be helpful to each other, they also had to confront such unpleasant facts as a certain physician's having a rather low reputation among his peers, or his having referred a patient too late to a specialist, or his having "dumped" an unattractive, chronically complaining patient into a colleague's lap, etc. Such facts crop up inevitably where real-life involvements exist. And it was in an attempt to cope with these facts—i.e., to prevent them from making the group's life and work unbearably difficult—that the group members resorted to certain myths or fictions—for example, to the myth that theirs was a particularly harmonious and well-matched group that far outclassed similar groups.

Because such group myths are at odds with a given group's reality, we could also call them fantasies. But when we do so, we need to distinguish these fantasies from those which we found to dominate groups of the Bion type. For the sake of clarity, I shall therefore continue to refer to them as myths.

However, it was not as group observer, but as family therapist that I came to appreciate the nature and central defensive role of such myths. And this is not surprising. For families are, after all, the opposites of ad hoc groups, as they share a common history and as their members have been and will be, fatefully and enduringly, enmeshed with each other.

This, in particular, holds true for children's involvements with their parents. (And here we must remind ourselves that even as parents we always remain children to our own parents.) For the children's style of thinking, acting, and loving, their capacity for enjoyment, their hopes, their readiness to trust and be trusted, and many more features are linked to what they experienced, or did not experience, in their family. By the same token, the parents' most basic satisfactions, as well as their deepest despairs, derive to a large extent from what did and does, or did not and does not, transpire in their relations with their children. It is, then, this *factuality* of family relations that makes family myths so important.[1][8]

Family myths, as here intended, have been extensively described and illustrated by A. Ferreira (1963) who emphasized their homeostatic function. He maintained that "the family myth is to the relationship what the defense is to the individual."

A CLASSIFICATION OF FAMILY MYTHS

Depending on their major defensive function, I distinguished between three types of family myths that I found to recur in certain disturbed families: (a) *myths of harmony*, (b) *myths of exculpation and redemption*, and (c) *myths of salvation*. In each case, the myths serve to blot out or selectively distort certain aspects and implications of the members' real past and present involvements with each other. They differ in their overall defensive thrust and chosen theme(s). Over time, though, these themes may shift or interweave, reflecting the fact that myths can change, evolve, or fade away in accord with changing defensive needs.

A. MYTHS OF FAMILY HARMONY

These myths paint a rosy picture of past and present family togetherness, family harmony, and happiness—in contrast to what a perceptive observer often notes within his first minutes of contact with such families. These are families who appear miserable, conflicted, depressed, or blandly bored, yet expressly believe, and try to make others believe, that they are the happiest and most harmonious families on earth. Here we find some of those pseudomutual families whom Wynne *et al.* (1958) have described. Their eager and "loving" friendliness with each other serves to blot out and dissociate past and present disagreements and hostilities. By employing myths of harmony, they cement the dissociation and throw unpleasant facts into the "memory hole," as described in Orwell's *1984*.

Jointly they rewrite the family history, just as Stalin's and Hitler's textbooks rewrote the histories of Russia and Germany. The distortions of historical facts can be similarly blatant. In one family, for example, the parents had on one occasion battered a child so severely that he needed surgical treatment. This was some 15 years before the family entered treatment. By this time, the members had created a myth of harmony that made such intrafamily brutality appear unreal and incomprehensible. The incident was unearthed only during the course of lengthy family therapy. Typically, the battered victim, no less than his victimizing parents, had shared in the construction and maintenance of this myth—i.e., had made it into a true myth of harmony.

B. MYTHS OF EXCULPATION AND REDEMPTION

These myths have a more complicated structure than the myths of harmony. In myths of harmony, the family members primarily employ the shared defenses of denial and idealization; in myths of exculpation and redemption they resort also to projective identification. A certain person (or persons), either inside or outside the family, either dead or alive, is jointly perceived to perpetrate (or have perpetrated) the family's badness, bad fortune, or misery. Hence he must exculpate the rest of the family as well as himself. He must serve as his family's delegate in the sense in which I have defined this term in this book and elsewhere (1972a, 1972d, 1973b, 1973c). As a delegate, he must, above all, allow the other members to observe *in him* their "disowned" badness or madness and to redeem, *through him*, their disowned guilt. Myths give a seeming coherence and rationality to this delegating process. This is partly analogous to the way in which the Jesus myth served to redeem and exculpate by proxy millions of Christian believers.

These myths, we note, differ from myths of harmony in that they take more seriously the factuality of the members' enduring involvements. For these myths imply an assessment and judgment of what the members did, or did not do, to each other. Through these myths, accounts are drawn up, and blame and fault are assigned. But such accounting becomes prematurely closed and slanted, as it were. The difficult and painful work of probing each member's merits and debits on ever deeper levels of interpersonal complexity, of facilitating an exploration and confrontation, and of a final reconciliation on the family level, remains undone.

Again we note that such myths, in order to be believable and workable, require the cooperation of all family members, including that of the victim-delegate. As I. Boszormenyi-Nagi (1972) has shown, this delegate may win as well as lose. By

allowing himself to become victimized, he can operate the guilt
lever on his parents—i.e., can enjoy psychological power over
them.

Myths of exculpation and redemption do not necessarily involve
an immediately available victim-delegate but may implicate an
absent or dead one, for example, a "bad" alcoholic father who is
no longer in sight. This father, so the myth goes, malevolently
deserted his faithful wife and loving children. Therefore he needs
to be shunned and castigated. It often takes much probing before
such notions can be recognized for what they are, namely myths,
the more so as the alleged perpetrator (and implied redeemer) of
the family's plight cannot account for himself in person.
Nonetheless, such myths can be corrected. Here I think
particularly of one family in which a "deserting" father was,
indeed, perceived as the cause of all family troubles. Al family
members shared in the belief that he was innately bad, corrupt,
irresponsible—in brief, the scum of the earth. This father's
"desertion" occurred approximately ten years before the family
entered therapy. Meanwhile, the mother had remarried. Her new
husband, the children's stepfather, had also come to believe that
the family's current difficulties—such as the mother's depression,
the oldest girl's promiscuity, the boy's school difficulties,
etc.—were essentially due to this father's desertion. Gradually,
though, this myth was punctured, as it became known that the
father's "desertion" was in part engineered by the mother who
then had a love affair with her boss. More and more this father
came to be seen not so much as an irresponsible runaway, but as a
pathetic evictee who again and again clamored to reenter the
family, yet each time was rebuffed.

C. MYTHS OF SALVATION

Myths of salvation extend the myths of exculpation and
redemption. Jesus, who took upon himself the sins of others,
promised not only redemption but also salvation—necessitating, in
turn, the additional myth of a paradisiacal state after death, to be
found in some heavenly Beyond, where all-loving and giving
parents (God and the Virgin Mother Mary) would provide a
happiness and approbation that somehow would render any
painful strivings, conflicts, and sufferings unnecessary. Salvation
myths on the family level are similar in essence. Here, too, we find
the shared belief that somehow the pains, conflicts, injustices, and

sufferings inherent in family life, and in the process of individuation and separation, can be avoided or undone through the benign intervention of some strong, if not omnipotent, figure or agency. Naturally, a family therapist, particularly when presenting himself with charismatic verve, may become and remain such a mythical person, the more so when his contacts with the family are brief and hence not subject to sobering disillusionments. In other cases, family members may jointly believe in the power and benevolence of some rich, good, strong, and caring relative or friend, such as an uncle or senator, who can lift them into some paradisiacal state where painful conflicts and efforts are not required.

These myths, like the others, thus serve to distort aspects and implications of the members' real past and present involvements with each other.

GROUP PROCESSES REVERBERATING WITH FAMILY PROCESSES

To succeed as his mother's delegate, Hitler, we saw earlier, had to resurrect his mother in Germany. Yet this, we realize now, involved complex group processes, which he tried to control but which also controlled him.

These group processes, I propose now, while partly unfolding under laws of their own, also implied, or reverberated with, typical family processes—processes that occurred on two levels primarily: one level referring to how the German people fared as individual family members; the other to how they viewed and defended their family of origin as system. And, on each level, Hitler's role was central.

On the first level, Hitler promised to resolve conflicts and undo damages that each German, as past and present family member, had suffered; on the second, he promised to repair, defend, and strengthen this German's cherished family image. On the first, he addressed individual, yet family-derived, frustrations, feelings of abandonment, vengeances, and hopes; on the second, he appealed to Germany as super-family, as *"Schicksalsgemeinschaft."* On the first, he played on primitive greed, sadistic, masochistic, as well as other normally censored wishes, as these evolved in family contexts; on the second, he upheld noble collective purposes. On the first, he enacted what Bion and others described as group fantasies; on the second, what I defined as family myths. For he espoused, first, a myth of harmony, envisioning *one Völk* that, relieved of all inner strife and totally *"ausgerichtet,"* spoke with one voice, felt with one heart, and marched to one tune. He espoused, second, a myth of exculpation and redemption, wherein one victim-delegate, the Jew, exculpated all other members and thus cemented their harmony; and he espoused, third, a myth of salvation that required him, Adolf Hitler, to act as Germany's lone savior.

HITLER AS DELEGATE OF THE GERMAN PEOPLE

Resonating with these multileveled processes, Hitler, I submit, came to act then not merely as his mother's delegate, but also as that of the German people. As such, he came to labor under missions which the Germans collectively, rather than his mother singly, entrusted to him, and which grew out of analogous family experiences. Let us, with this perspective in mind, once more consider Hitler's major missions, as earlier described.

The first was the mission to "give by receiving," i.e., to absorb his mother's regressive gratification and, in so doing, nurture her. As delegate of the German people, he became their super-nurturer, as it were. For, in reenacting the earlier symbiosis, he promised to give not only food and *Lebensraum*, but meaning, order, structure, everything—i.e., promised to fulfill dependency needs that were as primitive as they were total. Here Hitler's claim that he never erred resonated with the Germans' readiness to believe and obey him blindly, expressed in their *"Führer befiehl, wir folgen,"* ("Führer, give orders, we follow!")—two reciprocal attitudes that bolstered, as well as mirrored, a myth of harmony.

In the second mission, we found, Hitler had to redeem his mother's worth. It was primarily through this mission that he tried to absorb and undo her gravest trauma—the deaths of her first three children—and also the guilt and shame linked to it. As delegate of the German people, Hitler resonated here with an analogous trauma, suffered by the whole German nation: the sudden and seemingly inexplicable loss of the First World War and with it of her (Germany's) "children"—her provinces—at a time when the Germans still believed themselves to be victors and rightful masters of large conquered territories, particularly in the East. (The peace treaty of Brest-Litowsk, concluded in 1917 with Russia, had left them in control of vast expanses.) Binion has proposed and documented this perspective, in accord with the work of A. Hillgruber (1967) and other historians.[19]

On a national scale, the above mission fitted in with Hitler's third major one—to furnish his mother's life, through his exploits, with importance, excitement, and power by proxy. Through this mission Hitler also promised to wipe out Germany's shame and guilt, tuning himself to a mentality and milieu to which he had been exposed from his childhood on—that of the German petit bourgeois, or *Kleinbürger*, whose daily life consumed itself in dull routine, neighborhood gossip, meek subservience to unquestioned authorities, and beer hall patriotism (in German, *Stammtischgeschwätz*), contrasting starkly with the excitement, adventure, true comradeship, and heroism of war that Hitler—in fact *and* fantasy—was able to provide. For Hitler, according to Hjalmar Schacht (1949), "could play like a virtuoso on the well-tempered piano of lower middle class hearts."[20] Günter Grass' description in his novel, *The Tin Drum*, of how the lower middle class in Danzig, Grass' home town, responded to Hitler, portrays, I believe, the essence of Nazism.

Of course, Hitler did not act as the delegate of the lower middle class alone. All members of the German *"Völkgemeinschaft"* seemed to need him, not least its women. Masses of otherwise inconspicuous German housewives stood in the crowds that cheered him, eagerly delegating him to become the son, lover, husband, or father of whom their dreary reality deprived them. And Hitler obliged, as both charmer and despiser, while they, either solemnly or giddily, acted as his foster mothers and channeled onto him their unlived sexual longings, their needs to be aroused, abused and exploited, to be shown the path of duty, but also to be entertained with mighty, if bloody, spectacles. D. Eckard, one of Hitler's early "intellectual" mentors, well grasped what Hitler, as the German masses' thrill-providing delegate, had to be like:

We need a fellow at the head who can stand the sound of a machine gun. The rabble need to get fear into their pants. We can't use an officer, because the people don't respect them any more. The best would be a worker who knows how to talk. ... He doesn't need much brains, politics is the stupidest business in the world, and every marketwoman in Munich knows more than the people in Weimar. I'd rather have a vain monkey who can give the Reds a juicy answer, and doesn't run away when people begin swinging table legs, than a dozen learned professors. He must be a bachelor, then we'll get the women.[21]

There was, finally, Hitler's mission to serve as his mother's ally and avenger, i.e., to provoke, topple, and destroy a father whose power he feared and envied, and whose outward harshness and inward corruption and weakness he loathed. Here again, I believe, Hitler responded to what countless Germans experienced, and, her too, it seems, his mission fitted a shared national trauma. I have in mind the Germans' experience with President Wilson who, after powerfully intervening in the war, ended it with a promise of a fair peace, but who, seemingly distant, corrupt, and ineffective, could not live up to his promise and let Germany, mutilated and helpless, die in shame, as it were, just as Dr. Bloch had once mutilated and killed Hitler's mother.[22] Thus, he tapped a collective sense of injustice that he helped to transform into collective retaliatory fury, now displaced at another stand-in: the corrupt, international, poisonous Jew. Here he executed a mission which, at one and the same time, satisfied basest instincts and noblest aspirations and one that fitted both a myth of redemption and exculpation, and one of harmony.

WAS HITLER'S A TYPICAL GERMAN FAMILY?

With the above I assumed that Hitler's own family exemplified that of numerous Germans, holding similar formative experiences to result in similar—and resonating—character structures. I assumed, specifically, that there existed a common family scenario in which a submissive, restricted mother reeled under an outwardly domineering, but inherently weak and frequently distant, husband, and that this mother therefore massively bound and delegated her offspring who, in turn, would elicit the envious father's harsh retributions. And I assumed, further, that the offspring's ensuing character included two major features: an enduring willingness to reenact with "leaders" the earlier symbiosis—or, if you wish, bound-up-ness—and a peculiar mixture of massive frustrations and inner conflicts that would generate fierce destructiveness—aimed at the self, others, or both, if circumstances permitted.

I readily concede that these assumptions are open to doubt. For one thing, Hitler was not even a *Reichs* German, but a German-Austrian; for another, we lack, as yet, psychosocial studies that could convincingly prove or disprove such assumptions. Still, I believe, indirect evidence from various sources tends to corroborate them. Thus, we may turn to reports in the literature on typical, if minor, Nazis who were later psychoanalyzed, i.e., those run-of-the-mill Germans who once related to Hitler as delegators and delegates. Here I consider most important the insights that the psychoanalysts M. and A. Mitscherlich provide. In their book, *Die Unfähigkeit zu trauern* (*The Inability to Mourn*, 1967), these authors perceptively examine the minds and childhoods of average Nazis and thereby offer us a needed complement to my analysis of Hitler, especially as they also illuminate the families in which their patients grew up. The following brief formula on one of their patients aptly characterizes, I believe, many German delegator/delegates who resonated with Hitler: "As his mother's child he is a victim, as the father of his children he is a commander (*Befehlshaber*) if not persecutor, as a tyrannical husband of a willing spouse he is a strong he-man, as sexual partner who cannot satisfy her, he is the impotent weak male."[2 3]

E. H. Erikson, too, in his studies on Hitler's childhood in 1942 and 1950—while they adopt a vantage point partly different from mine and need updating in the light of recent research—tends to support the assumption that Hitler and his fellow Germans had comparable family experiences. Erikson finds in Hitler's, as well as in the *Reichs*-German, character, a "peculiar combination of idealistic rebellion and obedient submission" which in his view reflects "the exclusion of the individual fathers as an influence and the adherence to some mystic-romance entity: Nature, Fatherland, Art, Existence, etc., which were super-images of a pure mother"[2 4] and which points back to a basic family structure that is similar to, if not identical with, the one I outlined. Erikson links this family structure to a German conscience which "is self-denying and cruel; but its ideals are shifting and, as it were, homeless. The German is harsh with himself and with others; but extreme harshness without inner authority breeds bitterness, fear, and vindictiveness. Lacking coordinated ideals, the German is apt to approach with blind conviction, cruel self-denial, and supreme perfectionism many contradictory and outright destructive aims."[2 5] This conscience, I believe, is that of a bound delegate, as earlier defined, who suffers deep conflicts of missions as well as loyalties.

Another study, published only a few years ago, suggests that even today young Germans are more willing than young Americans or Englishmen to reenact, with "leaders," an earlier symbiosis. I have in mind the study of J. Adelson (1971) on the political imagination of the young adolescent, in which he compared about 450 adolescents from three nations—the United States, West Germany, and Great Britain—with each other.[2 6]

Adelson relied mainly on detailed interviews with adolescents in the age range from 11 to 18, of both sexes and of normal to extremely high intelligence, through the full spectrum of social classes. While his aim was "to discover how adolescents of different ages and circumstances construct the world of political action, and how they organize a political philosophy," he found that the German youths revealed a strong penchant to obediently accept authority and thereby recreate the earlier symbiotic bound-up-ness. To quote:

> The German interviews . . . are the easiest to grasp. The distinguishing themes can be stated boldly and simply. They are also familiar—eerily so. Reading some of these interviews—not all, but a substantial minority, perhaps 30 per cent of them—we feel ourselves drawn or thrown back thirty or forty years, to those sentiments about citizen, state, and society which we then took to be "uniquely" German. Despite at least two decades of successful democratic practice, despite the earnest attempt of most educated Germans to wash their hands of the past, much of that political spirit persists—as many observers have noted, and as our interviews made painfully plain. Consider the following statement by an eighteen-year-old German girl, responding to a question on the purpose of government. Nothing like it, nothing remotely like it, appears in the American or British interviews. "We have to have someone who takes responsibility for us, so that they don't become confused, the whole community, so that there's one person who governs us, and shares an interest in what we do and everything."

In this brief extract we catch a glimpse of several of the motifs that distinguish the German interviews: *the fear of confusion; the identification of government with a single person; and, above all, the view of authority as parental and of the citizen as a child. The governing power is seen as wise and benevolent, the citizen as weak and dependent, the two joining symbiotically.* Given this nuclear view of the political enterprise, most of the singular features of German political thought fall into place.

The ordinary citizen is seen as weak, or stupid, or incompetent. He does not know enough to come in out of the rain. A disdain for "the people" runs through the interviews: "people must all be guided somehow . . . they can't otherwise make sense out of what happens to them," "the laws are created because otherwise when one lives without laws . . . then one cannot tell if what one is doing is right."

Indeed, it is sometimes implied that stupidity, or a sheeplike docility, *should* be the proper state of mind for the citizen:

"[Laws are needed] so that all the people can live in such a way that they don't have to think about what's going to happen to them very much."

"There should be [a law forbidding smoking] because . . . otherwise people would have to decide for themselves if it's good or bad for their health or not."

They wanted to have a guiding principle that one could defer to without further ado, without reflecting on his deeds and considering whether something is correct or false.

These last quotations point to a recurrent theme in many of the German interviews: the anguish of ambiguity, the pain of deciding among alternatives. Ambiguity begets confusion, and confusion is an internal state most deeply feared. Out of the fear of ambiguity, and the deeper fear of confusion, of being adrift in a sea of possibilities, comes the need to reduce diversity, to seek order, clarity, and direction. Hence the German youngster turns to the strong leader. Without firm leadership, there will be chaos, anarchy.[27]

In sum, there is reason to believe that the family structure and shared character that underlay many a German's vulnerability to Hitler continue to exist.

MORE ON THE INABILITY TO MOURN

Hitler, I noted earlier, failed truly to mourn his mother, for he failed to confront and reexperience what tied him to his lost object: love, devotion, ambivalence, rage, and other emotions. Here, too, the Germans acted like Hitler. Rather than mourning *their* losses and confronting *their* pains, they tried to deny them with Hitler's help. And by acting in his participatory theatre and adopting his myths, they too compounded their problems as they, like Hitler, entwined themselves in expanding shame-guilt spirals. Thus it came about that all the sound and fury that the stagecrafter Hitler unleashed did, in the final analysis, signify nothing to them, as it left their original family problems unsolved and further burdened their offspring. For should my assumptions be valid—that the Germans' plight derived largely from fathers who were distant and corrupt, and from mothers who were closely binding and delegating—Hitler worsened their plight: he involved masses of absentee fathers in a criminal war and, at the same time, left their offspring more exposed than ever to tightly binding and delegating mothers. Many of these bound and delegated children, grown into adolescents and young adults, had to confront returning fathers who, rather than facing up to what they had done, preferred flimsy denials and thereby increased their children's contempt. Thus, the generations became locked into more tragic binds, as more fathers failed their sons in helping them to become fathers to a new generation. The unusually militant and self-destructive features of the present German student unrest derive, I believe, at least partly from this failure of the father-generation.[28] And so does the apparent need of many of these students to embrace, with uncompromising harshness, new myths of harmony, of exculpation and redemption, and of salvation, now frequently presented in Marxist garb.

TOWARD A FAIRER ACCOUNTING

Even though several decades have passed since Hitler's death, the task of drawing up accounts still looms large. Let me finish this essay by briefly commenting on it. What, I shall finally ask, can my family view of Hitler contribute?

Here we must distinguish between two types of role in Hitler's participatory theater—those who actively (albeit often covertly) acted as delegator-delegates, and those who were merely coerced. The former brought Hitler to power and, by their contributions, kept him there; the latter became victims of this power. The former constituted those German masses who, as his delegators, swept Hitler to increasingly radical feats and, as his delegates, executed his missions. They were thus not unlike the (more or less hidden) supporters of certain present-day terrorists. These terrorists murder innocent victims, yet as delegates of their largely invisible supporters (e.g., "the Arab masses"), they can stay free of guilt and view themselves as heroes or martyrs. But once Hitler was swept into power, the scenario changed. While he still required the German masses as his delegators or delegates—and found them willing, with very few exceptions, to serve him voluntarily if not enthusiastically—he now augmented his arsenal of stagecrafting assets by adding two that made a qualitative, as well as quantitative, difference: terror, and (seemingly) legitimate power. With them he could now coerce countless otherwise unreachable people—first and foremost the Jews of Europe but, in fact, all residents of countries that he invaded or challenged—to join him, chiefly as victims, in his participatory theater. Thus, in drawing accounts, we must here distinguish between two types of *dramatis personae:* actively, albeit often covertly, contributing delegator-delegates (i.e., the great majority of Germans) and coerced victims.

My chosen perspective bears mainly on the first type. While it makes Hitler more humanly understandable and may even—contrary to my intentions—seem to excuse him, it also permits us to grasp and assess, at least to an extent, what his delegator-delegates contributed. In this it differs, for example, from Fromm's perspective on Hitler, as outlined earlier, since Fromm, in focusing on Hitler's "necrophilous character," narrows, if he does not abort, the quest for accountability. His treatment of Speer seems paradigmatic here. He reassures us that Speer, whom he apparently came to know well, had changed completely since his days as Hitler's Minister of War Production.[29] This may be so; the fact remains, though, that it was largely due to Speer's efforts and formidable talents that the war stretched out for months, if not for years, that the carnage went on and millions of Jews died. In his own book, Speer (1970) registers this achievement with barely concealed pride.[30] Thus, even though Speer, with the assistance of Fromm and others, may now portray himself as a one-time naive technocrat and misguided idealist, we must nonetheless inquire not only into his actual cooperation with Hitler, but also into his erstwhile reading of *Mein Kampf,* which contains, in frank language, the reasoning, the moral principles, and the radicalism which Hitler, as Germany's Führer, enacted.

To conclude: the inability to mourn presupposes the inability—or unwillingness—to draw up accounts, i.e., to assess what each participant in Hitler's theater did or did not contribute. This, clearly, is a painful, difficult, and perhaps never-ending task. But to carry it on, we need, I believe, to view Hitler in a family perspective.

EPILOGUE

Was Hitler the most evil man there ever was? Last Sunday, my daughter and I returned to this question—yet reached no conclusions. Our talk started after we had both watched *The Great Dictator*, a film produced around the start of World War II, wherein Charlie Chaplin impersonated Hitler.

Will Charlie Chaplin's Hitler, I suddenly wondered, take hold of her imagination just as Peter von Heydebreck, mounted on his horse and trampling the roses, took hold of mine when I was her age? And would this, then, mean that her image of Hitler would forever fuse with that of a little man who bounces, struts, and raves, who performs funny tricks, and who, for some strange reason, commands huge crowds, wields enormous power, and kills millions of innocents?

As if to counteract such an image, I thought up a story for her which would begin somewhat as follows: "One day a baby called Adolf Hitler was born. There still exists a picture of that baby. It shows, as far as we can make out, a good baby, cuddly and with big eyes, such as most mothers would want. And his mother, whose name was Klara, wanted him badly. But then all went wrong and the baby grew up to become Hitler, whom many people believe to have been the most evil man there ever was."

Yet here I stopped myself because I realized I was merely repeating, in ways a child might understand, what I said in this book—which dealt, after all, mainly with Hitler's development, motivations, and relationships, not with his evil deeds.

To take account of these—and to answer my daughter's question—another book would have to be written. That book would first have to assess him as a man who, by his orders, caused unspeakable human suffering—had millions killed and maimed, additional millions driven from their homelands, their families disrupted, their cultural heritages destroyed, their hopes shattered. It would then have to assess him as an ideologue who, by his teachings, corrupted human minds and poisoned international relations—who held that it is right for some people who deem themselves elites to view other people, adults and children, as vermin to be exterminated. And it would finally have to assess him as a human model and leader to the family of German peoples.

This, then, brings me to a final insight that this book provides—one that draws on the similarities I find between family leaders (or therapists) and national leaders.

Here Hitler's qualities as a destructive leader to the German nation contrast with those which a constructive leader, within my family perspective, must have. For such a leader, I believe, rather than providing and abetting national or family myths, must foster a climate of exploration which finally makes them unnecessary. Rather than patching over and displacing conflicts and tensions, he must help the family or nation to contain and examine them. Rather than acting as stagecrafter and enactor of fantasies, he must help the members to endure reality. Rather than preventing their mourning, he must facilitate it. Rather than displaying charisma, vindictive passion, omniscience, and omnicompetence, he must show integrity, curiosity, and a readiness to admit, as well as learn from, mistakes; and, perhaps most important, he must act as an impartial arbiter who, guided by compassion and empathy, commits himself to seek "interpersonal justice."

Helm Stierlin, M.D., Ph.D.

NOTES

CHAPTER I: HITLER REVEALED AND CONCEALED

1. About the importance of *Lebensraum* (living space) in Hitler's political thinking, see R. Binion, 1973, p. 187.
2. B. F. Smith, 1967, p. 25.
3. *Ibid.*, pp. 41-42.
4. F. Jetzinger, 1956, p. 51.
5. B. F. Smith, 1967, pp. 44-45.
6. *Ibid.*, p. 43.
7. Based on a statement by Frau Rosalia Schichtl Hoerl, who worked as a cook and maid in the Hitler household during the latter part of 1884 and early 1885. See B. F. Smith, 1967, pp. 36-37.
8. Chart reprinted with permission of R. Binion, 1973, p. 207.
9. See B. F. Smith, 1967, p. 51. However, Binion, in a personal communication, believes that this is not documented for the newborn child. The contrary is more likely, as the only extant photograph of the baby Adolf shows an overfed, yet apparently healthy, baby.
10. This accords with how Paula Hitler described her parents and the relationship they had with each other. In her interview with John Toland, she reported that her father was "the absolute type of the old Austrian official, conservative and loyal to his emperor to the skin. My mother, however, was a very soft and tender person, the compensatory element between the almost too harsh father and the very lively children who perhaps were somewhat difficult to train. If there were ever quarrel [*sic*] or differences of opinion between my parents it was always on account of his children." (From the John Toland Collection.)
10a. *Hitler Source Book*, National Archives, Washington, D.C., pp. 924-930.
10b. *Ibid.*, p. 925.
10c. The John Toland Collection.
11. G. Kurth was the first to recognize the importance of this passage. Before she published her finding (1947), she had conveyed it to W. Langer who later incorporated it into his book (1972). More recently, N. Bromberg (1974) added one more argument for the autobiographic nature of the above statement: In further elaborating it in *Mein Kampf*, Hitler lapsed inadvertently and abruptly into the first person singular. Here Bromberg reminds us that Hitler, very likely,

dictated *Mein Kampf* in the Landsberg prison to Rudolf Hess in a manner that implied a stream of consciousness and evocation of childhood memories.

12. Quoted from *Mein Kampf*, pp. 31-32.
13. *Ibid.*, p. 28.
14. B. F. Smith, 1967, p. 52.
15. According to W. Maser (1971/1973), Alois, Jr. worked first as a waiter. Between 1900 and 1902, he was jailed twice for theft. In 1907 he worked in Paris; he left in 1909 for Ireland. During the twenties he lived in Germany where he drew a jail sentence for bigamy. Later he went to England, but returned at least once more to Germany in order to benefit from his halfbrother's prominence—in vain, as it turned out, since Adolf ignored him totally and even forbade the mention of Alois, Jr.'s name in his presence. While in Ireland, Alois, Jr. fathered a son, William Patrick Hitler. See W. Maser, 1973, p. 27n.
16. The evidence here is spotty, though, as he is also reported to have broken down on his father's bier. See W. Maser, 1971, p. 32.
17. J. C. Fest, 1973, pp. 37-39.
18. W. Maser, 1973, p. 51.
19. *Ibid.*, p. 40.
20. Handwritten account by Dr. Eduard Bloch, November 7, 1938. NSDAP Central Archives, Federal Archives, Koblenz, NS 26/65.
21. W. Maser, 1973, p. 41. Dr. Eduard Bloch is quoted (*Collier's*, 1941, p. 37), as follows, on this subject: "In the practice of my profession it is natural that I should have witnessed many scenes such as this one, yet none of them left me with quite the same impression. In all my career I have never seen anyone so prostrate with grief as Adolf Hitler."
22. B. F. Smith, 1967, p. 8.
23. *Ibid.*, pp. 8-9.
24. *Ibid.*, p. 9.
25. Smith (1967, p. 9) seems to assume here, along with many others, that we can make linear extrapolations from childhood and adolescent traits to adult traits, e.g., can assume or predict that a shy child will turn into a shy adult. This assumption, though, is increasingly questioned as a result of careful longitudinal studies. Cf. here particularly F. Jones (1974), J. Kagan and H. Moss (1962), and others.
26. N. Bromberg (1971) has written about Hitler's sexual habits: " . . . the only way in which he could get full sexual

satisfaction was to watch a young woman as she squatted over his head and urinated or defecated in his face." He also reports ". . . an episode of erotogenic masochism involving a young German actress at whose feet Hitler threw himself asking her to kick him. When she demurred, he pleaded with her to comply with his wish, heaping accusations on himself and grovelling at her feet in such an agonizing manner that she finally acceded. When she kicked him, he became excited and as she continued to kick him at his urging, he became increasingly excited. The difference in age between Hitler and the young women with whom he had any sexual involvement was usually close to the twenty-three years difference between his parents. From what we have seen about the sources for Hitler's sexual anxieties and his characteristic defence mechanisms, it is not too difficult to trace the emergence of his perversions. In the first place, his intense castration anxiety and fear of the female genitalia readily account for the preference to see rather than to act. Indeed, seeing itself is sexualized in his case, since the organs of sight are substitutes for parts of his genital apparatus, the testicles. Now, what is it that is so sexually stimulating for him to see. Roehm is quoted as having once said in Hitler's presence:

" 'He (Hitler) is thinking about the peasant girls. When they stand in the fields and bend down at their work so that you can see their behinds, that's what he likes, especially when they've got big round ones. That's Hitler's sex life. What a man!' This would give support to the surmise that it was not the—to him—frightening front view of the female vulva that intrigued Hitler, but the rear view. That, unlike the front view, would be reassuring, since not only would the fecal stick represent the penis, but also the lower portions of the labia visible behind it simulate the appearance of the testes. Thus, what he would see also resembled the topography of the male genitals seen from the front. The reassurance comes, of course, both from the absence of a sight that stimulates castration anxiety and from the identification with an object that actually seems to be possessed of a penis and testicles. This, in turn, leaves the way open for the sexual gratification derived from the masochistic humiliation meted out by the object's anal-sadistic befouling of the pervert" (pp. 300-301n).

27. Hitler's lack of one testis was noted by the Russian

pathologists who conducted the autopsy on his charred remains. See L. Bezymenski, 1968.

28. "Geli" Raubal's given name was Angela Marie.
29. R. Binion, 1973, pp. 208-209.
30. E. Fromm, 1973, p. 374.
31. *Ibid.*, p. 375.
32. *Ibid.*, p. 376.
33. *Ibid.*, p. 377.
34. *Ibid.*, p. 363.
35. *Ibid.*, p. 379.
36. *Ibid.*, p. 391.
37. *Ibid.*, p. 378.
38. See H. Picker, 1965.
39. *Ibid.*
40. E. Fromm, 1973, p. 401.
41. Fromm evidently relies here on Trevor-Roper (1947); the *Lagebesprechungen* (strategic deliberations) show it was not so. Cf. also N. Rich, 1973, 1974.
42. Other Hitler scholars do not share this view, as they noted an increasing breakdown of controls. See here especially Trevor-Roper (1947), G. Boldt (1964), J. Rectenwald (1963), and H. D. Rohrs (1966).
43. E. Fromm, 1973, p. 432.
44. R. Binion, 1973, p. 207.
45. Summarized by R. Binion, 1973, p. 192.
46. *Ibid.*
47. Quoted by Binion, p. 192.
48. *Ibid.* Stierlin's italics.
49. B. F. Smith, 1973, p. 224.
50. *Ibid*
51. R. Binion, 1973, p. 190.
52. Others who have singled out these as the two major thrusts of Hitler's politics include E. Jäckel (1972), A. Hillgruber (1967), and R. Bollmus (1970).
53. R. Payne, 1973, p. vi.

CHAPTER II: HITLER BOUND AND DELEGATED
             BY HIS MOTHER

1. G. Simmons, 1968, p. 154.
2. *Ibid.*, p. 151.
3. Personal communication from D. Reiss, 1970.
4. I am indebted to K. Ravenscroft, Jr. for this formulation.
5. For a particularly illuminating portrait of Vienna during the last decades of the Hapsburg Monarchy, see A. Janik and S. Toulmin, 1973.
6. See J. von Müllern-Schönhausen (no date), pp. 198-203. According to a personal communication from E. Jäckel, the evidence that von Müllern-Schönhausen offers is weak, consisting essentially of a registry that he reproduces. As Jäckel found von Müllern-Schönhausen to be unreliable—if not fraudulent—in other matters, caution seems indicated here.
7. N. Bromberg (1974) sees here "parallels to his son Adolf's later insistence on legitimacy, however brutally distorted, while seizing and using power," p. 230.
8. W. Maser, 1973, p. 4.
9. Bertolt Brecht's poem is translated by Stierlin.
10. B. F. Smith, 1967, p. 42.
11. P. Weissman, 1964, pp. 148-149.
12. *Ibid.*
12a. *Hitler Source Book*, NA, p. 925.
13. J. C. Fest, 1974, p. 19.
14. A. Kubizek, 1955. This portrait, however, is doubted by Binion and Jetzinger, for it conflicts with more reliable reports on Hitler as a youth; and Hitler's own correspondence with Kubizek shows no trace of such attacks either. According to Jetzinger (1956), this part of Kubizek's portrait of Adolf is fantasy. I tend to disagree with Jetzinger, though, because I find confirmation of at least some of these traits in Hitler's *Secret Conversations* (1953), particularly in pages to which I shall turn shortly. Hitler gives evidence here of an attacking and, it seems to me, self-destructive "rebelliousness" which also has anti-Semitic undercurrents.
15. Cf. here Hitler's own account of his student days in his *Secret Conversations* (1953), pp. 155-160.
16. Hindenburg actually resembled Alois and was *"der alte Herr"* for Hitler even in his chitchat of the early 1940s. Throughout his political career, Hitler approached Hindenburg in a deferential-resentful attitude, always

vacillating between the two poles of his ambivalence.

17. *Secret Conversations*, p. 160.
18. My profound thanks to Professor Eberhard Jäckel, from whom I received this as yet unpublished poem.
19. The use of the asterisk (*) indicates undecipherable parts of the poem: *Unleserlich; auch das übrige nur schwer leserlich;* all of it is difficult to read. Preliminary version, still to be checked by the Bundes Archiv.
20. Entry into the guest book of Schoibers Inn. Undated. The date derived from the preceding entry. Contains two sketches. Sent to the *Reichskanzlei* (Reichs Chancellery) in March 1941 from Friedrich Seids of Steyr. Cf. Table Talk of January 9, 1942, in Hitler's *Table Talk*, p. 193ff., and W. Maser (1971, p. 68n).
21. Last line of poem, literally translated: "And heals with beatings his wounds."
22. *Secret Conversations*, p. 159: "I remember the sort of quarrel they often used to have. A few days before, I had asked my landlady—politely—to give me my breakfast coffee a little less hot, so that I should have time to swallow it before we set off. On the morning of this quarrel, I pointed out to her that it was already half-past the hour, and I was still waiting for my coffee. She argued about whether it was so late. Then the husband intervened. 'Petronella,' he said, 'it's twenty-five to.' At this remark, made by someone who had no right to speak, she blew up. Evening came, and Petronella had not yet calmed down. On the contrary, the quarrel had reached its climax. The husband decided to leave the house, and, as usual, asked one of us to come with him—for he was afraid of the rats, and had to be shown a light. When he'd gone, Petronella bolted the door. Gustav and I said to one another: 'Look out for squalls.' The husband at once injured his nose on the shut door, and politely asked his wife to open. As she didn't react, except by humming, he ordered her to do as she was told, but without any better success. From threats he passed to the most humble supplication, and ended by addressing himself to me (who could only answer that his charming spouse had forbidden me to obey him). The result was that he spent the night out of doors, and could not return until next morning with the milk, pitiful and cowed. How Gustav and I despised the wet rag! Petronella was thirty-three years old. Her husband was bearded and ageless. He was a member of the minor nobility, and worked as an employee in the service of

the municipality."
23. See footnotes 49 and 50, in Chapter I.
24. See here particularly W. Greene, 1974.
25. A. Kubizek, 1955, p. 158.

CHAPTER III: HITLER AS CREATIVE AND DESTRUCTIVE ARTIST

1. N. Rich, 1973, p. xxxvi.
2. A. Koestler, 1968, p. 384.
3. W. Maser, 1971, pp. 57, 66.
4. *"Gesamtkunstwerk"* (a total work of art). See here also Hitler's enthusiasm for the works of Richard Wagner, reported by Kubizek (1955) and Fest (1973/1974).
5. A. Bullock, 1962, p. 68.
6. R. Binion, 1973, p. 192.
7. R. Binion, 1973, pp. 192, 210, quotes this by Ernst Hanfstaengl, in *Hitler Source Book*, N.A.
8. J. C. Fest, 1974, pp. 36-57.
9. *Der Stern* July 5, 1973.
10. R. Binion, 1973, p. 192.
11. *Mein Kampf*, pp. 212-213.
12. *Der Stern*, July 5, 1973.
13. See A. Speer's "Afterword" to J. Brosse's *Hitler Avant Hitler.*
14. See *Mein Kampf*, Chapter VI, pp. 176-186.
15. W. Maser, 1971, pp. 137-140.
16. This quote is found in *The Diary of Anaïs Nin*, 1969, p. 187.
17. Cf. A. Zoller (1949), p. 196, as quoted by J. C. Fest, 1973, p. 30.
18. J. C. Fest, 1973, p. 911.
19. See Fest, 1973, p. 996. However, Jäckel (1972), Rich (1973, 1974), and other historians do not share this view. Rather, they see Hitler as an empire builder who failed because he underestimated or miscalculated realistic obstacles.
20. R. Binion, 1973, p. 252.
21. H. Segal (1974) states that "The artist's compulsion to create may at times be overriding and ruthless. . . . There is a beautiful description of this aspect of creativity in Patrick White's *The Vivisector* (1970)." See H. Segal (1974), p. 139.
22. "Following a year in a psychiatric hospital (the Autenriethsche Klinik in Tübingen) he [Hölderlin] led a restricted life in a tower in the same city from 1807 until 1843, cared for by a carpenter by the name of Ernst Zimmer.

Hölderlin wrote only a few, relatively short, poems during these last ... years of his life. In their seemingly childlike simplicity they would never suggest to the uninitiated that they were written by one of Germany's greatest lyric poets" (Stierlin, 1972b, p. 193).

23. To Kafka, the snorts and wheezes of the tubercular patient evoked the image of a beast that " . . . bores its snout into the earth with one mighty push and tears out a great lump; while it is doing that I hear nothing; that is the pause; but then it draws in the air for the new push. This indrawal of its breath which must be an earth-shaking noise, not only because of the beast's strength, but also because of its haste, its furious lust for work as well; this noise I then hear as a faint whistling . . . day and night it goes on, boring with the same freshness and vigor always thinking of its object . . . compared with this what are all petty dangers in brooding over which I have spent all my life?" (Kafka, 1948, p. 209). Kafka, clearly, tried to obtain an advantage from his murderous illness by letting it generate a striking vision and by subjecting it to a penetrating psychological analysis; but in the end the "beast" won out over all of Kafka's efforts to analyze, tame, and contain it. For, as it burrowed deeper into his lungs, it sapped his vitality and destroyed his wish to struggle on, to seek independence, to marry. Finally, the only liberation he could envision was one of deep, regressive self-abdication—a liberation that amounted to a drif into nothingness and death. When his tuberculosis was diagnosed on September 4, 1917, he wrote to his publisher, Kurt Wolff: "My illness, allured for years by headaches and insomnia, suddenly broke out. It is almost a relief" (Kafka, 1958, p. 159). This happened to be the moment when Kafka, after a deep inner struggle, was finally to marry Felice Bauer. The sickness, noted his psychoanalytic biographer, John S. White (1967), now spared him this fateful act. It also allowed him to quit his position at the Workmen's Compensation Office, which he hated so much, and to go to live with his sister, Ottla, who managed a little rural boarding house in Zürau near Saatz. Hence, the feeling of inner liberation, of quasi euphoria, that overcame him when he finally met his illness head on! The illness came at a time in his life when he was to undertake what he held to be the most decisive step toward maturity. But rather than taking this step, he let himself, under the disguise of outer necessity, drift into passivity and ever deeper dependent boundness. He derived from his tuberculosis, so he told Felice, "the kind of

immence support a child gets from clinging to its mother's skirts" (Kafka, 1973, p. 545). And there was Ottla, a stand-in for his mother, ready to provide all the regressive gratification he could wish. "Ottla," he wrote, "carried me so to speak on her wings, through a difficult world ... the room is ... excellent ... all I am supposed to eat is here in big quantity and good quality (only the lips refuse it in a spasm but this always happens in the first days of change) and the *freedom*, most of all, the *freedom*" (Kafka, 1958, p. 161). But, clearly, this freedom was no longer the one he had hoped to achieve through the creative process. Most of the above can be found in my paper, "Liberation and Self-Destruction in the Creative Process," to be published as a chapter in *Janus*, Louis L. Orlin (Ed.), by the Center for Coördination of Ancient and Modern Studies, University of Michigan, at Ann Arbor.

CHAPTER IV: SHAME, GUILT, VENGEFULNESS, AND LOYALTY IN HITLER'S MOTIVATIONS

1. Here I disagree with W. Treber (1966) who diagnosed Hitler as schizophrenic. Treber adopts here the position of a distant observer typical of many German psychiatrists brought up in the Kraepelinian tradition. Regarding the diagnosis of schizophrenia see my works on that subject (1958, 1964, 1967).
2. F. Alexander (1963) speaks mostly of "feelings of inferiority," where other authors, such as G. Piers and M. Singer (1953), H. M. Lynd (1961), and H. B. Lewis (1971), speak of "feelings of shame." Also see my paper on the subject of shame and guilt (1974a).
3. Envy, more than other emotions, seems to have simultaneous links to guilt *and* shame, particularly in children. For a person often feels that envy is destructive to others, as well as being deeply humiliating to himself.
4. G. Piers and M. Singer, 1953, p. 11.
5. Also see my paper (1974a) which deals in more detail with the dynamics of shame.
6. J. C. Fest, 1974, p. 517.
7. *Ibid.*, pp. 517-518. Also see *Hitlers Tischgespräche im Führerhauptquartier [Hitler's Table Talk in the Fuhrer's Headquarters] 1941-1942*, edited by H. Picker (1951), p. 433; and A. Zoller, 1949, p. 126.
8. J. C. Fest, 1974, p. 518.

9. H. Picker, 1951, p. 170; also see *Mein Kampf*, p. 70.
10. R. Payne, 1973, pp. 281-282.
11. H. Stierlin, 1959.
12. G. Piers and M. Singer (1953), H. Ward (1972), H. B. Lewis (1971), and my paper on the subject of shame and guilt (1974a).
13. *Jenseits von Gut und Böse*, Aphorism 108, Nietzsche, 1954.
14. F. Alexander, 1963, p. 126.
15. Nietzsche, Aphorism 78.
16. *Ibid.*, Aphorism 98.
17. E. Erikson, 1968, especially Chapters 7-9.
18. D. W. Winnicott, 1958, p. 96.
19. R. Binion, 1973, p. 192.
20. I. Boszormenyi-Nagy and G. Spark (1973) introduced this concept into the family literature. Central here is the notion that each member keeps account of what he gave and what he received from all other family members, and what he therefore owes or is due (e.g., love, attention, sacrifice, etc.). To an extent, this bookkeeping operates out of awareness. Family therapy, according to the authors, aims at making the "ledger of merits" explicit and at newly assessing and possibly renegotiating the members' reciprocal contributions.
21. Quoted by R. Payne, 1973.
22. H. Picker (1965), as quoted by E. Fromm, 1973, p. 400.
23. There exists by now an enormous literature on the nature and pathology of the mourning process. Besides S. Freud's seminal "Mourning and Melancholia" (1917), I refer the reader to E. Lindemann (1944), R. Wetmore (1963), N. Paul and G. Grosser (1965); also to the works of C. M. Parkes (1964, 1965a, b, 1970), D. Maddison (1968) and, with his co-workers (1967, 1968).

CHAPTER V: HITLER AND HIS FOLLOWERS:
A VIEW ON GROUP DYNAMICS

1. In many respects, the pre-Hitler Weimar also spawned an impressive culture. But many of its elements seem to have abetted rather than impeded Hitler's rise to power. See P. Gay (1968).
2. Cf. E. H. Erikson (1942).
3. The Prussian and German constitution, in contrast to that of other Western powers, allowed the king to play a decisive role as long as he had a compliant Chancellor. For its fundamental principle was "that the Chancellor of the German Empire and

Prime Minister of the Prussian Crown depended upon the confidence of the Emperor and King. So long as he enjoyed this confidence he could not be removed from his office, not even by vote of Parliament. This was the basic axiom of the German constitutional system, as envisaged by Stahl and executed by Bismarck, the *differentia specifica* which distinguished it from the parliamentary systems of Western Europe" (E. Eyck, 1967, p. 17).

4. *Mein Kampf*, p. 180.
5. See G. Kurth, 1947.
6. *Mein Kampf*, p. 366.
7. *Mein Kampf*, p. 118.
8. *Mein Kampf*, p. 356.
9. *Mein Kampf*, pp. 337-338.
10. *Mein Kampf*, p. 381.
11. S. Freud, 1914, p. 101.
12. Quoted by R. Manvell and H. Frankel, 1968, pp. 146-147.
13. P. Turquet, 1974, p. 358.
14. *Ibid.*, p. 35.
15. Here the contributions of L. deMause (1974), G. S. Gibbard (1974), G. S. Gibbard and J. H. Hartman (1973a, 1973b, 1973c), J. H. Hartman (1971), J. H. Hartman and G. S. Gibbard (1973), E. Jaques (1948, 1953, 1955, 1974), R. D. Mann (1959, 1966, and, with others, 1967), A. K. Rice (1963, 1969), P. Slater (1955, 1966, 1974), and G. S. Gibbard, J. H. Hartman, and R. D. Mann (1974), among others, are outstanding.
16. L. deMause, 1974, in conversation.
17. Also see the works of M. Klein (1946, 1957), R. Fairbairn (1954), and Harry Guntrip (1971).
18. Such factuality does not exclude certain fantasies from playing important roles in the members' involvements with each other. In fact, such involvements often imply that other members are exploitatively recruited via projective identification and other processes. These others must here "embody" those "bad" fantasies the recruiter needs to disown, yet also needs to keep in a close "working distance" to himself. These "fantasy phenomena," as occurring on the intrafamily level, are part of the reality of exploitation that I subsume under the term "factuality of family relations."
19. R. Binion, 1973, pp. 250-251.
20. H. Schacht, 1949, p. 206, as quoted by A. Bullock.
21. Quoted by Konrad Heiden in *Mein Kampf*, p. 687n2.
22. Consider here, for example, a speech which Hitler gave on

March 4, 1920, entitled "The Truth about the Brutal Truce [*Gewaltfrieden*] of Brest-Litowsk and the So-called Truce of Reconciliation and Understanding of Versailles." Here Hitler, according to the extant PND report, asserted: "Four of our warring enemies concluded peace treaties with us. We Germans, who are overwhelmingly honest and well-meaning people, believed in Wilson's promises for a peace of reconciliation and were so bitterly deceived. Instead of reconciliation—deceit, instead of fair negotiations—brute power. Comparison: the armistice of Brest-Litowsk, as concluded by us (not 3 of 1000 Germans know it) [massive applause] and the armistice of Versailles that was forced on us." Hitler went on to compare the two treaties in detail, each time emphasizing the injustice of the Versailles treaty. (PND report M35, Copy S&A Nürnberg, Polizeidirektion Nürnberg-Fürth. Nr. 550. From an unpublished collection of documents on Hitler, compiled by E. Jäckel and A. Kuhn.)

23. A. and M. Mitscherlich, 1967, p. 51. (Stierlin's translation.)
24. E. H. Erikson, 1950, p. 335.
25. *Ibid.*, pp. 335-336.
26. Consider here also the classical studies by T. W. Adorno, *et al.* on *The Authoritarian Personality* (1950), as well as those of E. C. Devereux, U. Bronfenbrenner, and G. J. Suci (1962).
27. J. Adelson, 1971, pp. 1038-1040. (Italics in second paragraph are Stierlin's.)
28. At the same time, they derive from the upsurge of revolutionary attempts, of group solidarity, and of utopian fantasies as these invariably follow a decay in the deification of leaders. See G. S. Gibbard and J. H. Hartman (1973).
29. At one point Fromm even analyzes a dream of Speer's—not with a view as to what it says about Speer, but about Hitler. Also see G. Barraclough, 1971.
30. Consider here, for example, how Speer (1971) describes his meeting with General F. L. Anderson, commander of the bombers of the American Eighth Air Force, while he (Speer) waited for his arraignment as war criminal: "Our guard of soldiers from a German armored force presented arms (even after the cease-fire, the German troops around Doenitz's government seat were allowed to bear light arms. At this meeting I stated, according to the minutes for May 19, 1945, that 'I have no need of collecting credits in order to avert misinterpretations of my actions. The political aspects will be examined by other quarters.'), and so—under the protection

of German arms, as it were—General F. L. Anderson, commander of the bombers of the American Eighth Air Force, entered my apartment. He thanked me in the most courteous fashion for taking part in these discussions. "For three days more we went systematically through the various aspects of the war in the air. On May 19 Chairman Franklin d'Olier of the USSBS, along with his vice-chairman, Henry C. Alexander, and his assistants, Dr. Galbraith, Paul Nitze, George Ball, Colonel Gilkrest, and Williams, visited. From my own work I could appreciate the great importance of this division for the American military operations. During the next several days an almost comradely tone prevailed in our 'university of bombing.' It came to a sudden end when Goering's champagne breakfast with General Patton produced banner headlines all over the world. But before that happened General Anderson paid me the most curious and flattering compliment of my career: 'Had I known what this man was achieving, I would have sent out the entire American Eighth Air Force merely to put him underground'. That air force had at its disposal more than two thousand heavy daylight bombers. I was lucky General Anderson found out too late" (p. 629).

Bibliography

Adelson, J. "The political imagination of the young adolescent." *Daedalus, Twelve to Sixteen: Early Adolescence,* 100: 1013-1050, 1971.

Adorno, T.W., Fränkel-Brunswick, E., Levinson, D.J., and Sanford, R.N. *The Authoritarian Personality.* New York: 1950.

Alexander, F. *Fundamentals of Psychoanalysis.* New York: 1963.

Barraclough, G. "Hitler's Master Builder," *New York Review of Books,* January 7, 1971, 6-15.

Bateson, G. "Double Bind," Symposium address, Annual Meeting of the American Psychological Association, Washington, D.C., September, 1969.

Bateson, G., Jackson, D., Haley, J., and Weakland, J. "Toward a theory of schizophrenia," *Behavioral Science,* 1:251-264, 1956. —"A note on the double bind," *Family Process,* 2: 154-161, 1963.

Bezymenski, L. "The Death of Adolf Hitler," *Unknown Documents from Soviet Archives.* New York: 1968.

Binion, R. *Frau Lou.* Princeton (New Jersey): 1968.

— "Hitler's concept of *Lebensraum:* The psychological basis," *History of Childhood Quarterly,* 1: 187-215, 1973.

— "Reply to Commentaries on Symposium Article," *History of Childhood Quarterly,* 1: 249-258, 1973.

Bion, W.R. "Experiences in Groups: I," *Human Relations,* 1: 314-320, 1948.

— "Experiences in Groups: II," *Human Relations,* 1: 487-496, 1948.

— "Group dynamics: A review," *Int. J. Psycho-Anal.,* 33: 235-247, 1952.

— *Experiences in Groups.* New York, London: 1959/1961.

Bloch, E. (as told to J.D. Ratcliff). "My Patient, Hitler," *Colliers Magazine,* 15. March, 1941.

Blos, P. *On Adolescence: A Psychoanalytic Interpretation.* New York: 1962.

— *The Young Adolescent. Clinical Studies.* New York: 1970.

Boldt, G. *Die letzten Tage der Reichskanzlei.* Hamburg: 1964.

Bollmus, R. *Das Amt Rosenberg und seine Gegner.* Stuttgart: 1970.

Boszormenyi-Nagy, I. "Loyalty implications of the transference model in psychotherapy," *Arch. Gen. Psychiat.,* 27: 374-380, 1972.

— and Spark, G.: *Invisible Loyalties: Reciprocity in Intergenerational Family Therapy.* New York: 1973.

Bromberg, N. "Hitler's character and its development: Further observations," *American Imago*, 28: 289-303, 1971.

— "Hitler's childhood," *Int. Rev. Psycho-Anal.*, 1: 227-244, 1974.

Brosse, J. *Hitler avant Hitler. Essai d'interpretation psychoanalique.* Paris: 1972.

Bruch, H. "Falsification of bodily needs and body concepts in schizophrenia," *Arch. Gen. Psychiat.*, 6: 18-24, 1962.

Bullock, A. *Hitler, A Study in Tyranny.* New York: 1964.

deMause, L., Editor. *The History of Childhood.* New York: 1974.

Domarus, M. *Hitler, Reden und Proklamationen 1932-1945.* Würzburg: 1962/63.

Devereux, E. C., Bronfenbrenner, J., and Suci, G.J. "Patterns of parental behavior in the United States of America and the Federal Republic of Germany: A cross-national comparison," *Int. Social Science J.*, 14: 488-506, 1962.

Eliade, M. *Myth and Reality.* New York: 1968.

Erikson, E. H. "Hitler's imagery and German youth," *Psychiatry*, 5: 475-494, 1942.

— *Childhood and Society.* New York: 1950.

— *Identity and the Life Cycle.* New York: 1959.

— *Identity, Youth and Crisis.* New York: 1968.

Eyck, E. *A History of the Weimar Republic. Vol. I. From the Collapse of the Empire to Hindenburg's Election.* New York: 1962/1967.

— *A History of the Weimar Republic. Vol. II. From the Locarno Conference to Hitler's Seizure of Power.* New York: 1963/1967.

Fairbairn, W. R. D. *An Object-Relations Theory of Personality.* New York: 1954.

Fenichel, O. *The Psychoanalytic Theory of Neurosis.* New York: 1945.

— "Early Stages of Ego Development." *Collected Papers of Otto Fenichel.* New York: 1954, 25-48.

Ferreira, A. "Family myths and homeostasis," *Arch. Gen. Psychiat.*, 9: 457-463, 1963.

Fest, J. C. *Hitler. Eine Biographie.* Frankfurt/Berlin/Vienna: 1973.

Freud, A. *The Ego and the Mechanisms of Defense.* New York: 1946.

Freud, S. *Zur Einführung des Narzißmus. Ges. Werke* 10: 137-170, London: 1946.

— *Trauer und Melancholie. Ges. Werke* 10: 427-446, London: 1946.

— *Das Ich und das Es. Ges. Werke* 13: 235-289, London: 1940.

— *Hemmung, Symptom und Angst. Ges. Werke* 14: 111-205; London: 1948.

Fromm, E. *The Anatomy of Human Destructiveness.* New York/Chicago/San Francisco: 1973.

Gay, P. *Weimar Culture. The Outsider as Insider.* New York: 1968.

Gibbard, G. S. "Individuation, Fusion, and Role Specialization," G. S. Gibbard, J. H. Hartmann, and R. D. Mann Editors: *Analysis of Groups*, San Francisco/Washington/London: 1974.

— and Hartmann, J.J. "Relationship patterns in self-analytic group," *Behavioral Science*, 18: 335-353, 1973 (a).

— "The significance of utopian fantasies in small groups," *Int. J. Group Psychother.*, 23: 125-147, 1973(b).

— "The oedipal paradigm in group development: A clinical and empirical study," *Small Group Behavior*, 23: 305-354, 1973(c).

Grass, G. *Die Blechtrommel.* Neuwied: 1959.

Greene, W. A. "Role of a vicarious object in the adaptation to object loss," *Psychosomatic Medicine*, 20 344-350, 1958.

Guntrip, H. *Psychoanalytic Theory, Therapy, and the Self.* New York: 1971.

Haley, Jr. "The family of the schizophrenic: A model system," *J. Nerv. Ment. Dis.*, 129: 357-374, 1959.

Hanfstaengl, E. *Zwischen Weißem and Braunem Haus.* Munich: 1970.

Hartmann, J. J. "The case conference as a reflection of unconscious patient-therapist interaction," *Contemporary Psychoanalysis*, 8: 1-17, 1971.

— and Gibbard, G. S. "The bisexual fantasy and group process," *Contemporary Psychoanalysis*, 9: 303-322, 1973.

Hillgruber, A. *Deutschlands Rolle in der Vorgeschichte der beiden Weltkriege.* Göttingen: 1967.

Hitler, A. *Mein Kampf.* Munich: 1935.

— *Hitlers Zweites Buch. Ein Dokument von 1928.* Stuttgart: 1961.

— *Hitler's Table Talk.* 1941-1944. London: 1953. Translated as *Hitler's Secret Conversations.* New York: 1953.

— *Hitlers Lagebesprechungen. Die Protokollfragmente seiner militärischen Konferenzen.* Edited by H. Heiber. Stuttgart: 1961.

Jäckel, E. *Hitlers Weltanschauung.* Tübingen: 1969.

Janik, A., and Toulmin, S. *Wittgenstein's Vienna.* New York: 1973.

Janouch, G. *Conversations with Kafka. Notes and Reminiscences.* New York: 1971.

Jaques, E. "Interpretive group discussion as a method of facilitating social change," *Human Relations*, 1: 533-549, 1948.

— *The Changing Culture of a Factory.* London: 1951.

— "On the dynamics of social structure," *Human Relations*, 6:

3-24, 1953.

— "Social Systems as a Defense Against Persecutory and Depressive Anxiety," M. Klein, P. Heimann, and R. E. Money-Kryle editors: *New Directions in Psychoanalysis.* New York: 1955, 478-498.

Jetzinger, F. *Hitlers Jugend. Phantasien, Lügen—und die Wahrheit.* Vienna: 1956. (English version: *Hitler's youth.* Translated by Lawrence Wilson. London: 1958.)

Johnson, A., and Szurek, S. A. "The genesis of antisocial acting out in children and adults," *Psychoanal. Quart.,* 21: 323-343, 1952.

Jones, F. H. "A four-year follow-up of vulnerable adolescents: The prediction of outcomes in early adulthood from measures of social competence, coping style, and overall level of psychopathology," *J. Nerv. Ment. Dis.,* 159: 20-30, 1974.

Kafka, F. *Letters.* New York: 1958.

— *Diary. 1910-1923,* New York: 1948.

— *Sämtliche Erzählungen.* Edited by P. Raabe. Frankfurt: 1970.

Kagan, J. and Moss, H. *From Birth to Maturity: A Study in Psychological Development.* New York/London: 1962.

Kekulé, A. *Theoretical Organic Chemistry. Papers Presented to the Kekulé Symposium.* London: 1959.

Klein, M. *New Directions in Psycho-Analysis.* New York: 1956.

— *Envy and Gratitude.* New York: 1957.

— "Our Adult World and its Roots in Infancy," *Our Adult World,* New York: 1963, 1-22.

Koestler, A. *Darkness at Noon.* New York: 1941.

— *The Ghost in the Machine.* New York: 1968.

Kohut, H. *The Analysis of the Self.* New York: 1972.

Kubizek, A. *Adolf Hitler, mein Jugendfreund.* Graz—Göttingen: 1953.

Kurth, G. M. "The Jew and Adolf Hitler," *Psychoanal. Quart.,* 16: 11-32, 1947.

— "Hitler's Two Germanies. A Sidelight on Nationalism," *Psychoanalysis and the Social Sciences.* Vol. II. New York: 1950, 293-312.

Laing, R. D. "Mystification, Confusion, and Conflict," I. Boszormenyi-Nagy and J. L. Framo Editors: *Intensive Family Therapy.* New York: 1965, pp. 343-364.

Langer, W. C. *The Mind of Adolf Hitler. The Secret Wartime Report.* New York: 1972.

Le Bon, G. *The Crowd.* New York: 1960.

Lewis, H. B. *Shame and Guilt in Neurosis.* New York: 1971.

Lidz, T. *The Origin and Treatment of Schizophrenic Disorders.*

New York: 1973.
— and Cornelison, A. R., Singer, M. T., Schafer, S., and Fleck, S.
"The Mothers of Schizophrenic Patients," *Schizophrenia and the Family.* New York: 1965.
Lindemann, E.: "Symptomatology and management of acute grief," *Am. J. Psychiat.*, 101: 141-153, 1944.
Lüthy, H. *Nach dem Untergang des Abendlandes.* Köln, Berlin: 1964.
Lynd, H. M. *On Shame and the Search for Identity.* New York: 1961.
Maddison, D. "The relevance of conjugal bereavement for preventive psychiatry," *Brit. J. Med. Psychol.*, 41: 223-233, 1968.
— and Viola, A. "The health of widows in the year following bereavement," *Journal of Psychosomatic Research.*, 12: 297-306, 1968.
— and Walker, W. L. "Further studies in conjugal bereavement." *Aust. and N.Z. Journal of Psychiatry*, 63-66, 1969.
Mann, R. D. "A review of the relationship between personality and performance in small groups," *Psychological Bulletin*, 56: 241-270, 1959.
— "The development of the member-trainer relationship in self-analytic groups," *Human Relations*, 19: 85-115, 1966.
— and Gibbard, G. S., and Hartman, J. J. *Interpersonal Styles and Group development.* New York: Wiley, 1967.
Maser, W. *Hitler's Mein Kampf. An Analysis.* London: 1970.
— *Hitler: Legende, Mythos, Wirklichkeit.* Munich and Eßlingen 1971. (English translation, P. and B. Ross: *Hitler: Legend, Myth and Reality.* New York/Evanston/San Francisco/London 1973.)
Mitscherlich, A. and M. *Die Unfähigkeit zu trauern.* Munich: 1967.
von Müllern-Schönhausen, J. *Die Lösung des Rätsels Adolf Hitler. Der Versuch einer Deutung der geheimnisvollsten Erscheinung der Weltgeschichte.* Vienna.
Nin, A. *The Diary of Anais Nin, Vol III: 1939-1944.* Edited and prefaced by G. Stuhlmann. New York: 1969.
Nietzsche, F. *Werke in drei Bänden.* Munich: 1954.
Parkes, C. M. "Effects of bereavement on physical and mental health, study of the medical records of widows," *Brit. Med. J.*, 2:274-279, 1964.
— "Bereavement and mental illness. Part 1. A clinical study of the grief of bereaved psychiatric patients," *Brit. J. Med. Psychol.*, 38: -12, 1965(a).
— "Bereavement and mental illness. Part 2., A classification of bereavement reaction," *Brit. J. Med. Psychol.*, 38: 13-26,

1965(b).
— "The first year of bereavement. A longitudinal study of the reaction of London widows to the deaths of their husbands," *Psychiatry*, 33: 444-467, 1970.

Paul, N. and Grosser, G. "Operational mourning and its role in conjoint family therapy," *Community Mental Health J.*, 1: 339-345, 1965.

Payne, R. *The Life and Death of Adolf Hitler.* New York/Washington; 973.

Picker, H. *Hitlers Tischgespräche im Führerhauptquartier.* Stuttgart: 1965.

Piers, G. and Singer, M. *Shame and Guilt: A Psycho-Analytic and a Cultural Study.* Springfield, Illinois: 1953.

Rectenwald, J. *Woran hat Hitler gelitten?* Munich/Basel: 1963.

Reiss, D. *Persönliche Mitteilung,* 1970.

Rice, A. K. *The Enterprise and Its Environment.* London: 1963.
— "Individual, group, and intergroup processes," *Human Relations*, 22: 565-584, 1969.

Rich, N. *Hitler's War Aims. Ideology, the Nazi State, and the Course of Expansion.* New York: 1973.
— *Hitler's War Aims. The Establishment of the New Order.* New York: 1974.

Rohrs, H. D. *Hitlers Krankheit/Tatsachen und Legenden.* Neckargemünd: 1966.

Schacht, H. *Abrechnung mit Hitler.* Hamburg: 1948. (English translation, *Accounts Settled.* London: 1949.)

Searles, H. *Collected Papers on Schizophrenia and Related Subjects.* New York: 1956.

Segal, H. "Delusion and artistic creativity: Some reflexions on reading *The Spire* by William Golding," *Int. Rev. Psycho-Anal.*, 1: 135-141, 1974.

Simmons, G. *Barbarian Europe.* New York: 1968.

Singer, M. T. and Wynne, L. C. "Thought disorder and family relations of schizophrenics. III: Methodology using projective techniques," *Arch. gen. Psychiat.*, 12: 187-200, 1965.
— "Thought disorder and family relations of schizophrenics. IV: Results and implications," *Arch. Ge. Psychiat.*, 12: 201-212, 1965.

Slater, P. E. "Role differentiation in small groups," *Am. Sociological Rev.*, 20: 194-211, 1955.
— *Microcosm: structural, psychological and Religious Evolution in Groups.* New York/London/Sydney: 1966.
— "Some Problems Regarding Exemplification," G. S. Gibbard, J. J. Hartman, and R. D. Mann editors. *Analysis of groups.* San

Francisco/Washington/London: 1974.

Smith, B. F. *Adolf Hitler: His Family, Childhood and Youth.* Stanford: 1967.

—"Comment to Rudolph Binion's Symposium Article," *History of Childhood Quarterly*, 1: 221-229, 1973.

Speer, A. *Erinnerungen.* Berlin: 1969.

Stierlin, H. "Contrasting attitudes toward the psychoses in Europe and in the United States," *Psychiatry*, 21: 141-147, 1958.

— "The adaptation to the stronger person's reality," *Psychiatry*, 22: 143-152, 1959.

— "Bleuler's concept of schizophrenia in the light of our present experience," Third International Symposium on the Psychotherapy of schizophrenia, Lausanne, 1964, 42-53.

—"Bleuler's concept of schizophrenia. A confusing heritage," *Am. J. Psychiat.*, 123: 996-1001, 1967.

— *Conflict and Reconcilation.* New York: 1969.

— *Das Tun des Einen ist das Tun des Anderen.* Frankfurt: 1971.

— "Family dynamics and separation patterns of potential schizophrenics," D. Rubinstein and Y. O. Alanen editors. *Proceedings of the Fourth International Symposium on Psychotherapy of Schizophrenia.* Amsterdam, Excerpta Medica, 1972(a), 169-179.

— "Lyrical Creativity and Schizophrenic Psychosis as Reflected in Friedrich Hölderlin's Fate," E. E. George Editor. *Friedrich Hölderlin, An Early Modern.* Ann Arbor: 1972 (b), 192-215.

— "The Impact of Relational Vicissitudes on the Life Course Of One Schizophrenic Quadruplet," A. R. Kaplan Editor. *Genetic Factors in Schizophrenia.* Springfield, Illinois: 1972(c), 451-463.

— and Ravenscroft, K. Jr. "Varieties of adolescent separation conflict," *Brit. J. Med. Psychol*, 45: 299-313, 1972(d).

— "A family perspective on adolescent runaways," *Arch. Gen. Psychiat.*, 29: 56-62, 1973(a).

—"Group fantasies and family myths, some theoretical and practical aspects," *Family Process*, 12; 111-125, 1973(b).

— "Interpersonal aspects of internalizations," *Int. J. Psycho-Anal.*, 54: 203-213, 1973(c).

— "The adolescent as delegate of his parents," *Aust. and N.Z.J. Psychiat.*, 7: 249-256, 1973(b).

— and Levi, L. D., and Savard R. J. "Centrifugal versus centripetal separation in adolescence: Two patterns and some of their implications," S. Feinstein and P. Giovacchini Editors. *Annals of American Society for Adolescent Psychiatry. Vol. II. Development and Clinical Studies.* New York: 1973(e),

211-239.

— "Vicissitudes of Liberation and the Creative Process," Address at "Symposium on Literature and Psychology," University of Michigan Center for Coordination of Ancient & Modern Studies, Ann Arbor, Michigan, November-December 1973(f).

— "Shame and guilt in family relations: Theoretical and clinical aspects," *Arch. Gen. Psychiat.*, 30: 381-389, 1974(a)

— "Karl Jasper's psychiatry in the light of his basic philosophical position," *J. Hist. Behav. Sci.*, 10: 213-226, 1974(b).

— *Separating Parents and Adolescents. A Perspective on Running Away, Schizophrenia, and Waywardness.* New York: 1974(c).

— "Psychoanalytic approaches to schizophrenia in the light of a family model," *Int. Rev. Psycho-Anal.*, 1: 169-178, 1974(d).

— "Family Theory: An Introduction," A. Burton, editor. *Operational Theories of Personality.* New York: 1974(e), pp. 278-307.

Toland, J. *The John Toland Collection.*

Treher, W. *Hitler, Steiner, Schreber/Ein Beitrag zur Phänomenologie des kranken Geistes.* Emmendingen: 1966.

Trevor-Roper, H. R. *The Last Days of Hitler.* New York: 1947.

— "Lügen um Hitlers Leiche," *Der Monat*, 8: 3-12, 1956.

Turquet, P. "Bion's Theory of Small Groups," address at the National Institute of Mental Health, Bethesda, Maryland, June, 1965.

— "Four Lectures: The Bion Hypothesis: The Work Group and the Basic Assumption Group," address at the National Institute of Mental Health, Bethesda, Maryland, May 26, May 28, June 2 and June 6, 1971.

— "Leadership: The Individual and the Group," G. S. Gibbard, J. J. Hartman, and R. D. Mann editors. *Analysis of Groups.* San Francisco/Washington London: 1974, pp. 349-371.

Waite, R. G. L. *Hitler and Nazi Germany.* New York: 1965.

— "Adolf Hitler's Anti-Semitism: A Study in History and Psychoanalysis," F. F. Wolman editor. *The Psychoanalytic Interpretation of History.* New York/London: 1971

Ward, H. "Shame—a necessity for growth in therapy," *Am. J. psychother.*, 26: 232-243, 1972.

Weissman, P. "Why Booth Killed Lincoln. A Psychoanalytical Study of Historical Tragedy," N. Kiell editor. *Psychological Studies of Famous Americans. The Civil War Era.* New York: 1964.

Wetmore, R. J. "The role of grief in psycho-analysis," *Int. J. Psycho-Anal.*, 44: 97-103, 1963.

White, J. S. "Psyche and tuberculosis: The libido organization of

Franz Kafka," *The Psychoanal. Study of Society*, 4: 185-251, 1967.

White, P. *The Vivisector.* London; 1970.

Winnicott, D. W. "Transitional objects and transitional phenomena," *Int. J. Psycho-Anal.*, 34; 89-97, 1953.

— "Aggression in relation to Emotional Development," *Collected Papers.* New York: 1958, 204-218.

— "The location of cultural experience," *Int. J. psycho-Anal.*, 48: 3 8-372, 1967.

Wynne, L. C. and Singer, M. T. "Thought disorder and family relations of schizophrenics. I. A research strategy," *Arch. Gen. Psychiat.*, 9: 191-198, 1963(a).

— "Thought disorder and family relations of schizophrenics. II. A Classification of forms of thinking," *Arch. gen. Psychiat.*, 9: 199-206, 1963.

—and Ryckoff, I. M., Day, J., and Hirsh, S. I. "Pseudomutuality in the family relations of schizophrenics," *Psychiatry*, 21: 205-220, 1958.

Zoller, A. *Hitler Privat. Erlebnisbericht seiner Geheimsekretärin.* Düsseldorf: 1949.